Loitering at the Gate to Eternity

Memoirs of a Psychic Bystander

LOUISA OAKLEY GREEN

iUniverse LLC
Bloomington

LOITERING AT THE GATE TO ETERNITY
MEMOIRS OF A PSYCHIC BYSTANDER

iUniverse books may be ordered through booksellers or by contacting:

iUniverse
1663 Liberty Drive
Bloomington, IN 47403
www.iuniverse.com
1-800-Authors (1-800-288-4677)

ISBN: 978-1-4759-8875-8 (sc)
ISBN: 978-1-4759-8876-5 (hc)
ISBN: 978-1-4759-8877-2 (e)

Library of Congress Control Number: 2013907959

Printed in the United States of America.

iUniverse rev. date: 7/15/2013

Psi has been shown to exist in thousands of experiments. There are disagreements over how to interpret the evidence, but the fact is that virtually all scientists who have studied the evidence, including the hard-nosed skeptics, now agree that something interesting is going on that merits scientific attention.

—Dean Radin, PhD, *The Conscious Universe: The Scientific Truth of Psychic Phenomena*

TABLE OF CONTENTS

Part II: Psychic Friends and Strangers

Foreword

Fate's Sense of Humor

I first met Stephen and Louisa in 2008, when I was promoting my first book, *Do Dead People Watch You Shower?* Stephen was the assistant manager of a local mall bookstore and helped me out by setting up a book signing there. I could immediately tell that he was one of those rare, hard-working individuals with a truly good heart—and very handsome to boot!

I met Stephen's wife, Louisa, when she came to the front of the line with my book in her hands and asked me if, while signing it, I'd mind giving her a minireading. She had an incredible aura of intelligence around her. I was not surprised later on when I discovered she'd been a professional writer for several decades, covering a variety of genres from humor to heavy science to mysticism—the subject of this book. Her interests in life have also been quite eclectic. She delved into biology and anatomy in support of her medical writing, spent a year studying homeopathy, took two years to learn classical astrology online from the Faculty of Astrological Studies in London, maintained her own organic garden, performed pro bono writing for environmental causes, and, oh yes, raised two lovely daughters.

When she first met her husband, Louisa thought that paranormal accounts were nothing short of ignorant superstition. Perhaps that's why fate, with its usual sense of humor, paired her with someone as deeply psychic as Stephen. Fortunately, she is open-minded, and as the years went by, she slowly changed her opinion about the paranormal world. I was delighted when I learned that she had finally decided to write about her experiences as a "psychic bystander" surrounded by prescient family, friends, and strangers. I am happy to be one of them.

Louisa has two laudable goals she hopes to achieve with this book. First, she wants her readers to appreciate how common psychic ability is in the general population. It seems rare, because most people are reluctant to talk about it for fear of how others will react. As a result, a very mundane talent is erroneously thought of as being extraordinary. Second, she hopes that by sharing everyday paranormal experiences from a cross section of people, that readers who are grieving or who fear death will derive some comfort within these pages. Of course, those of us who are mediums know that death is like walking from one room into another, and that the other side is quite real.

By the time this is published, I will have four books in the marketplace that have shared the tales of people whom I have connected with loved ones on the other side. *Loitering at the Gate to Eternity* wonderfully dovetails with my efforts to share this inspiring reality with others. What makes this book unique is that it is written from the perspective of someone who professes not to be terribly psychic, but who is honoring the experiences of others through her journalistic talents.

From my perspective, everyone possesses an innate intuition, but some people open up to it more naturally than others. I would encourage everyone who reads this book to recognize in themselves their own psychic abilities and celebrate them. The more you seek them out, the more you will see them. I can tell you from experience that being in touch with your intuitive self will not only enrich your life but also make you a happier person!

Warmest regards,

Concetta Bertoldi
Psychic Medium, Author
March 2013

PREFACE

DANCING SKELETONS

If you cannot get rid of the family skeleton, you may as well make it dance.

—George Bernard Shaw, Irish playwright (1856–1950)

More than twenty years ago, I unwittingly married into a family of gregarious psychics spanning three generations (now four). It wasn't something they did for a living. They all had normal occupations and left their sixth sense at home. As the years went by, I also found myself increasingly surrounded by friends and healers who had similar amazing abilities. Oddly enough, this great gift seemed for the most part to have passed me over, making me feel like a psychic bystander.

This book wasn't planned—it just happened. One day I woke up and decided to start writing down stories about my husband Stephen's forty years of psychic experiences. Then, like a pebble tossed into a pond, chapters began rippling out over several months. When I finished writing down Stephen's tales, my interviews expanded to include his family. The next concentric circle consisted of our friends, who then suggested other friends.

The people whose experiences live in these pages hail from all walks of life, from business executives and teachers to retail employees. Their ages range from eleven to ninety-nine. Many call the East Coast their home; one lives as far away as England.

Through their generous sharing of personal stories, these gifted family members and friends helped me create this book. Some were quite comfortable with recounting their paranormal romps, while others were nervous about mentioning them, lest they be ridiculed.

To preserve privacy, only first names are used, except in the case of the psychic professionals who are mentioned in chapter 9. (They, obviously, are quite comfortable with their gifts.) All of their tales have been faithfully rendered sans embellishment.

Without these dear souls and their spiritual insights, eccentric humor, and unflagging compassion, how dull and one-dimensional my world would be! I love them all and am thankful to be surrounded by their light.

Acknowledgments

Invisible Helping Hands

The seventeenth century English poet John Donne once wrote, "No man is an island"—all people and situations are interconnected. Nothing happens by itself. The same applies to books. Behind every book is a network of invisible helping hands smoothing the writer's way on her literary path. I am acknowledging those unseen accomplices here.

My first and most ardent supporter was the woman who started me on my way—my mother, Louise, who taught me how to write. A close second was my father, Alfred, who stressed the value of education. He always told me, "It's more important for a woman to get an education than a man" (a ground-breaking comment from a man born in 1918).

I would also like to thank my husband and confidant, Stephen; daughter, Chelsea; and close friends, Zoë Elva Putnam, Debi Sussman, Jo Panzino, and Kim Dentzer, all of whom read through my first drafts and offered constructive comments. In addition, a colleague, Suzanne Gaby-Biegel, suggested I add interview questions exploring how those who shared their stories felt about their psychic beliefs—a valuable perspective.

Finally, as this is my first book, I would be remiss in not expressing my appreciation to freelance copyeditor Karen Sullivan and the support staff at my publisher, led by the intrepid coordinator Rebekka Potter, sage editorial consultant George Nedeff, and the all-knowing editorial services associates Rita Kelly and Holly Hess.

The journey of having this book published has been a pleasant one, thanks to all of you!

Louisa Oakley Green
April 2013

Introduction

The Psychic Cheat Sheet

There are more things in heaven and earth, Horatio, than are dreamt of in your philosophy.
—*Hamlet*, William Shakespeare, English playwright (1564–1616)

In the early 1940s, when my late mother-in-law, Connie, was growing up in Jersey City, New Jersey, her mother once told her and her three siblings not to leave the house. She said if they did, one of them would get hurt. Connie's mom, Grandma Dolores, was psychic—a gift that ran through the Italian side of my husband's family. A typical ten-year-old child, Connie resented her mom for always being right, so she went out anyway.

Unfortunately, that day as she was walking along the top ledge of a wall, Connie fell and dislocated her shoulder. Not wanting to allow her mother any satisfaction, she tried to cover it up and endured the pain silently through dinner that night. One can only imagine how excruciating sitting through that meal must have been. Finally, she confessed, validating her mom's prediction.

Many people think that psychic phenomena are nonsense. I certainly had my doubts before I met my husband and his prescient family. But when you live with mystics, you begin to soften in your skepticism.

A few summers ago my husband, Stephen, was up late at his computer, writing and surfing the Internet. Due to insomnia, he remained at his desk into the early hours of the morning. Over a period of several hours he began to develop tightness in his chest and was having difficulty breathing, which was unusual for him. About six o'clock in the morning, Stephen came upstairs to tell me that he wasn't feeling well. Eventually, we decided to get him some fresh air at a park nearby. As we walked around a small lake, his breathing became more labored, so we sat down on a bench. His chest pain increased, and I nervously suggested a quick ride to the local emergency room. He resisted, and suddenly at 8:15 a.m. all of the pain stopped and was replaced with an immense feeling of physical and emotional relief. His health restored, we returned home. Five minutes after we got in the door, the phone rang.

Stephen's father, Leo, had been staying in Connecticut with his girlfriend, Jill, and her family. Jill's daughter was calling to say that Leo had experienced difficulty breathing that morning, suffered a heart attack, and died in the ambulance on the way to the hospital. The time of death was 8:15 a.m. Stephen was shocked on two levels: he was stunned to hear his father had died, and now he understood that he had shared in his father's final moments on earth. When my husband received his father's watch from the hospital, there was an additional surprise: it was frozen at 8:15. The timepiece had inexplicably stopped at the instant of his father's death.

It's been said that everyone possesses psychic ability, but some people seem to have a more natural affinity for it than others. In her 2008 book *The ESP Enigma: The Scientific Case for Psychic Phenomena*, former Harvard Medical School professor Diane Hennacy Powell, MD, reported that some researchers believe genetics may be behind psychic ability—something which appears evident in my husband's family. She additionally suggested that psychic abilities might even represent a step forward in the brain's continuing evolution.

Not everyone who possesses outstanding psychic ability is born with it, though. Sometimes a traumatic event may bring it about. It can develop after a serious illness or injury, as it did with well-known medium George Anderson and noted Dutch psychic Peter Hurkos. It may occur following a near-death experience, as happened with Joe McMoneagle, who worked in the US Army's Psychic Intelligence Unit at Fort Meade, Maryland, for ten years. These types of events, Powell posits, may change the structure and function of the brain.

Altered brains may have abilities that normal brains do not, Powell adds. Einstein thought of the space-time continuum as a place where all time coexists, meaning that the past, present, and future all exist at once. The "normal" brain is set up to experience time as a series of linear moments. Hypothetically, without the linear constraints of the brain, which may be weaker in psychics and mediums, it may be possible to see across time into the past or future.

Experiments at the Stanford Research Institute in Menlo Park, California, found that psychic ability is increased in an environment in which electromagnetic radiation is blocked. Researchers measured this by placing subjects in Faraday cages, an environment that blocks electromagnetic radiation.

Scientists have long been fascinated with psychic phenomena. Duke University in Durham, North Carolina, established a psychic research facility in 1935, which eventually moved to an off-campus location, where it remains today. The founder, botanist Dr. Joseph B. Rhine, turned to parapsychology research after his college professor and mentor at the University of Chicago shared a personal account of an intriguing paranormal experience. In a film interview Dr. Rhine recounted his mentor's story, which took place in the 1920s.

As the story goes, a young couple who lived near the professor knocked on his door—many people didn't have telephones in those days—to ask a favor. The woman had experienced a disturbing, vivid dream the night before in which she saw her brother go into his barn and shoot himself in the head. She was, understandably, so

Psychic Research Institutions

- Boundary Institute, Saratoga, California

- Consciousness Research Laboratory, University of Nevada, Las Vegas (merged into the Institute of Noetic Sciences in 2001)

- Division of Perceptual Studies, University of Virginia, Charlottesville

- Institute of Noetic Sciences, Petaluma, California (founded in 1973 by Apollo 14 astronaut Edgar Mitchell)

- Mind-Matter Unification Project, Cambridge University, United Kingdom

- Princeton Engineering Anomalies Research Lab, Princeton University, Princeton, New Jersey (merged into the International Consciousness Research Laboratories in 2007)

- Stanford Research Institute International, Menlo Park, California

- Rhine Research Center, Durham, North Carolina

distraught by this vision that she wanted to go to his farm to make sure all was well. She asked the professor to drive them there. When they arrived, they walked into the barn and found her brother just as she had seen him in her dream: dead of a gunshot wound to the head. From the moment he heard that tale, Dr. Rhine became obsessed with establishing a scientific explanation for what had happened.

Today the Rhine Research Center is respected as a facility that scientifically conducts parapsychology and consciousness studies. They have unmasked psychic frauds as well as validated genuine psychic events. Joining that institution are many other prominent research facilities, universities, and governmental organizations worldwide that take psychic abilities seriously enough to funnel millions of dollars into them for ongoing research.

So if you think there might be something to clairvoyance and mediumship, you're not alone. My husband's family serves as a living example. The following story illustrates an instance when their preternatural gifts spilled over to the psychically challenged side of the family.

My father had passed, and we were planning his funeral. Feeling sentimental, we decided to call the minister who had led our church congregation when I was growing up. It had been many years since we had attended that house of worship, so our memory of the minister there was frozen in time. Little did we know that the good reverend had long since retired, was well into his eighties, and was now somewhat eccentric.

We met at the funeral home, an old colonial man-

The funeral home where Dad's wake took place.

sion filled with the overly sweet cologne of flower arrangements wafting on stale currents of perpetual air conditioning. At one point during the wake, the minister asked everyone to be seated for a brief service. I sat down in the front row between my mother and husband, bracing for tears. Then something peculiar happened that broke the tension of the moment.

During his eulogy, the minister rambled on aimlessly, leaving us stranded with the gradual and oddly amusing epiphany that he had lost his focus. As his monologue wandered about, I remember my husband leaning over and whispering that he saw my father standing next to the minister and impatiently tapping his foot. (My father was not known for his patience.) I didn't think much of it until my brother-in-law, Tom, contacted me a week later. He had delayed calling to avoid upsetting me on the day of my father's funeral. He wanted me to know that during the eulogy he had seen my father standing by the minister, arms crossed and impatiently tapping his foot.

This introduction has described the stories of both psychics and mediums. As you read through this book, it will be helpful to understand the distinction between these two paranormal types. Psychics are people who can sense things they shouldn't ordinarily know in the past, present, or future (like Grandma Dolores); mediums are people who can see and/or communicate with the dead (like Stephen and Tom). Some people have both abilities, and they're referred to as psychic mediums.

The research and autobiographical observations I've read about psychics and mediums indicate that they tend to be deeply emotional and creative (the famous psychic healer/photographer Edgar Cayce was a noted example). Among the people I interviewed for this book are writers, graphic artists, teachers, a nurse, business owners, sales managers, licensed massage therapists (LMTs), a retired nuclear power plant foreman, retail workers, and a retired administrative assistant. Many of these people, if not already working in a creative career, are involved in such activities as music, fine art, writing, or the performing arts.

So, is *everyone* who claims to be a psychic gifted with outstanding clairvoyance or mediumship? Probably not. Does psychic ability really exist, despite numerous frauds? Apparently so, at least according to several prestigious public, private, and military research facilities around the globe.

This is all fine with me. Much of the work I've done in my career as a writer has been in the scientific arena. But through the years I've learned that science only explains *how* things work; it doesn't answer the more profound question of *why* anything exists in the first place.

I like the idea that some people may have a psychic cheat sheet on life—that there may be an unseen world beyond, as populated and quirky as the one in which we live, filled with a flurry of invisible, opinionated, and nosy relatives and friends. I invite you to read the psychic tales that follow and decide for yourself.

PART I

PSYCHIC BLOODLINE

Psychic ability has a tendency to follow genetic bloodlines. When I began interviewing my husband's family members, I had no idea how many of them would end up yielding anecdotes for this book. But one interview led to another, as everyone I spoke with suggested yet another relative who had stories—so many, in fact, that they populate the first half of this book. Part I begins with Stephen's ancestors then recounts more than forty years of stories from Stephen and his brother Tom and his family. It is followed by my side, the skeptical and paranormally challenged psychic bystanders.

Psychic Family Tree*

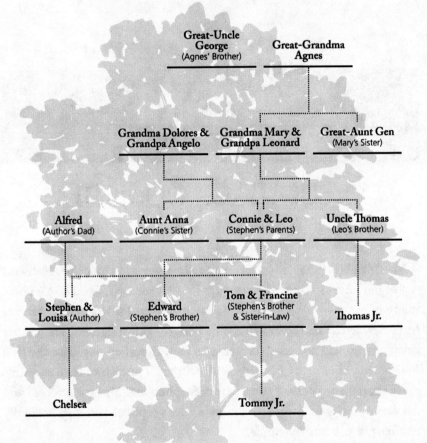

Great-Uncle George (Agnes' Brother) — Great-Grandma Agnes

Grandma Dolores & Grandpa Angelo — Grandma Mary & Grandpa Leonard — Great-Aunt Gen (Mary's Sister)

Alfred (Author's Dad) — Aunt Anna (Connie's Sister) — Connie & Leo (Stephen's Parents) — Uncle Thomas (Leo's Brother)

Stephen & Louisa (Author) — Edward (Stephen's Brother) — Tom & Francine (Stephen's Brother & Sister-in-Law) — Thomas Jr.

Chelsea — Tommy Jr.

*Partial tree: only lists family members mentioned in this book.

CHAPTER 1

ANCESTRAL DREAMS, OMENS, AND HAUNTINGS

Trust the dreams, for in them is hidden the gate to eternity.
—Khalil Gibran, Lebanese American artist/writer (1883–1931)

Before sharing the stories of my husband, Stephen, I thought it would be helpful to review some family reminiscences about his psychic ancestors, beginning with the heart of the Italian side of his family, Grandma Dolores. Most of their stories are brief, but they offer a glimpse into what it is like to live in a psychic family.

Dolores

Grandma Dolores was born in San Marco dei Cavoti, Italy, in 1909. I remember Dolores as a sturdy, gray-haired woman under five feet in height, with a sweet, heavily accented voice and a smile that exuded love. She possessed that wonderful combination of adversity-forged strength and unconditional nurturing common in Italian women.

Dolores married her husband, Angelo, when she was nineteen, and they had four children: Tony, Connie, Teddy, and Anna.

1

Sleeping "Telegrams"

Dolores was best known within the family for the psychic messages she received in her sleep. She would wake up from her prognostic dreams and jump into action to alert relatives and friends about a foreseen event. In one instance during the 1970s, she woke up and insisted that her younger daughter, Stephen's aunt Anna, call their cousin Mario. Mario was a tall, muscular man who had begun working in construction as a teenager and eventually established his own company several towns away. The family hadn't seen him in a while, but Dolores told Anna that something was horribly wrong.

She was right.

Mario had a son, Nick. Nick had been an active child. Because he was born with a clubfoot, he had endured several surgeries and much teasing at school. As a young adult, however, he was finally coming into his own. He was in college and had found a nice girlfriend.

When Anna called, Mario was startled at the timing. He was just about to notify the family of some terrible news. A driver had cut his son's car off in traffic, resulting in a serious accident. Nick was in the hospital in critical condition. Ten days later he passed away.

Spilt Milk

Over her life Dolores had multiple premonitions that one of her children would get hurt, and she tried her best to persuade fate to take another route. You may recall that she had predicted her daughter Connie's injury that resulted in a dislocated shoulder. Aunt Anna remembers another time when a similar warning bell went off in Dolores's sleep.

"Mom wouldn't let any of us kids out to play or do anything, because she had a dream someone was going to get hurt. She was positive of it," Anna said, noting that her older sister Connie was about nine years old at the time. "Mom took Connie to the store with her, thinking she would be safe. At the time milk bottles were made of glass. While Connie was carrying one, she tripped, fell, and cut her face on the broken glass. She needed quite a few stitches."

Thankfully, because Connie was so young, it healed well, leaving just a small scar on her face.

"So even though Mom was really careful, her dream did come true,"

Anna said. "I was very young, yet I remember it. We were mad because we couldn't go outside to play. But she was adamant about what this dream had foretold and didn't relent. Unfortunately, she could only foresee the event, not prevent it."

> **The Power of Dreams**
>
> Dreams are universal to the human experience. So it's no wonder that throughout history and in many cultures, dreams have been tools for divining the future, healing the sick, and enhancing spirituality. The earliest description of a prophetic dream was written more than three thousand years ago in a poem from Mesopotamia titled *The Epic of Gilgamesh*. In it, symbolic dreams foretold many events for the main character. In ancient Egypt and Greece, the sick or troubled sought cures to their woes by sleeping in special temples where priests interpreted their dreams. In the early Muslim tradition, "true dreams" were seen as a way God guided the faithful. And in sixteenth century China, *The Lofty Principles of Dream Interpretation* by Chen Shiyuan was considered an indispensable guide for translating dreams into meaningful messages.

Anna

Anna was the youngest of Dolores's four children, and she is the only one still living. She is a tough, spunky brunette with the mischievous ways sometimes exhibited by the baby of a family. She is also an inheritor of the family's psychic ability, something that has both helped and mystified her throughout her more than seven decades of life.

Aunt Anna serves as maid of honor at big sister Connie's wedding.

Aspirations in Blue

Career counseling can come from many sources, but the following one will probably not appear in any books containing vocational advice.

When Anna was single back in the 1960s, she met a young man who complained to her about his work. He felt stuck and unhappy in what he was doing. She blurted out without thinking, "Why didn't you become a cop like you originally wanted to?"

The man eyed her in disbelief. After all, they'd just met. Where did she get that information? More curious was the fact that she was absolutely right. He had wanted to join the force. He asked her how she possibly could have known that he aspired to be a police officer. She didn't have an answer—she just knew.

Bootie Alerts

When she wasn't offering career tips, Anna provided early warnings on incoming family members. One such alert went out to her older sister Connie.

After Connie delivered two sons, Stephen and Edward, she decided that her family was big enough. It was time to save up for a house. To ensure that she would stop at two children, she quietly practiced birth control.

So when Anna declared, "You're pregnant!" Connie felt confident that her smart-alecky younger sister was wrong.

The next week Connie went to see her doctor, who confirmed she was going to have a baby. The following year, Connie's youngest son, Tom, was born—a sweet little bundle of "I told you so."

How old were you when you had your first psychic experience?

"I was about eighteen or nineteen years old when it stood out and I realized other people didn't have the same ability. It made me more aware. When I got these feelings, I went with them, rather than fluffing them off. If I felt I didn't like someone, there was a reason for it, and usually I was right."

—Anna

Disarming Offspring

Children do the cutest things, but they have no sense of personal peril. As a result, parents spend a lot of time saving their little darlings from themselves. Having psychic ability would be extremely helpful to any parent—and in Anna's case, it was.

At about the same time her nephew, Tom, was born, Anna had her hands full with her own three-year-old son Angelo. One morning, when she was in her upstairs bedroom putting on her makeup, Anna felt a pang of panic. She dropped everything and dashed downstairs, unsure of what she would find. There, in the middle of the kitchen floor, was her precocious toddler smiling and holding a large, gleaming knife—terribly cute, terribly dangerous. She took the cutlery away from Angelo before he hurt himself. Fortunately her second sight had given her a heads-up on his mischief.

Good and Bad Premonitions

Premonitions offer a peek into an event that is about to happen. Larry Dossey, MD, reports in his book *The Power of Premonitions* that they generally fall into one of two categories: warning about something negative, such as illness, or heralding positive events, such as a new job. People can experience premonitions in a waking or sleeping state.

Genevieve

Great-Aunt Genevieve, whose nickname is Gen, lives in Pennsylvania coal-mining country and belongs to the paternal Polish side of Stephen's family. She's a spirited, plainspoken woman who has seen many mysterious predictions come to pass in her eighty-five years. One of them is illustrated in the following tale.

Great-Aunt Gen poses in a serious trench coat.

5

Harbinger

Fate played a central role in how one of Gen's favorite uncles both lived and died.

Gen's uncle Albert, whose nickname was George, heeded the call to join the military in the Great War (later renamed World War I). He was sent to the trenches somewhere in Europe, where more than a million men fought side by side in a war of bloody attrition from 1914 to 1918.

"He was drafted," Gen said. "Everybody was. Why else would they go?" Before he joined the army, Uncle George had never ventured farther from his home than he could walk. He was an outgoing young man who had a close relationship with his brothers, but all that changed after the war.

When he returned home in 1918, he was shell-shocked, suffering from what is now called post-traumatic stress syndrome, and experiencing epileptic seizures.

"When he came back, he was a different man," Gen said. "He kept to himself. He wasn't like that before he left. He had been a strapping, healthy young man full of life."

How old were you when you had your first psychic experience?

"When I was about seven or eight, I first heard about the owls crying out when somebody was about to die. It always happened. I'm a religious person, and I accept things as they are. A flower blooms one day, and before you know it, it's gone. We're all born to die."
—Gen

After the war Uncle George was never able to hold a job. Instead he was the family handyman, doing odd jobs around the house. He lived in the attic of the house next door to Gen with his sister, Agnes (Gen's mother), his niece Helen, and Helen's husband and small daughter. It was not unusual for several generations to live in one house and for extended families to live next door to each other.

Life was hard for coalminers and their families, and death was no stranger to them. Gen said that one well-known harbinger of the Grim Reaper was when an owl would perch on a tree near a person's home and cry out.

"Owls always cry before someone dies; they sense death," Gen said. "People used to try to chase them away by throwing rocks at the trees."

If any of Gen's relatives had tried that scare tactic one fateful night in 1934, it didn't deter the bird from its dark mission. During the evening, an owl perched near the family's house, crying mournfully. Uncle George died at three o'clock the next morning. In an ominous twist, the family noticed that the owl didn't go away, which puzzled them. The next evening it was still there, intoning a melancholic "hooo." Helen went into labor and was driven to the hospital to have a baby, but all did not go well. She died in childbirth. Following her death, the nocturnal predator was gone.

George poses in his uniform.

"The baby survived. Helen left behind two young girls," Gen said. Fortunately there was plenty of family around to help raise them. Still, the house must have felt achingly empty with the sudden departure of the quiet war veteran and the young wife and mother who was his niece.

Birds of Death

In the ancient cultures of Egypt, India, China, Japan, and some tribes of Central and North America, owls were considered the bird of death. In ancient Rome, in particular, the deaths of many famous people, such as Julius Caesar, were said to have been heralded by the hoot of an owl. David Johnson of the Global Owl Project hypothesizes that because owls often nest in cemeteries, where trees are left to grow undisturbed, that might be a factor in why they became associated with mortality. Following a millennium of dark reputation, it's not surprising that owls wended their way into coal-mining lore as harbingers of death.

Thomas

Stephen's late father, Leo, has one surviving brother, Thomas. As Great-Aunt Gen's nephew, he is also part of the Polish side of the family. Thomas, now retired, worked as a technician and foreman at a nuclear power plant. While he hasn't had many psychic experiences, he does remember a few.

Fruit Flies

Apples have symbolized various things across many cultures. In the Bible eating one led to problems in the Garden of Eden.* In the world of science one fell on Newton's head and is said to

Uncle Thomas relaxes at a family gathering.

---

*Never read an unpublished manuscript to your mother. A Bible scholar, she insisted I clarify that Genesis never said Eve ate an apple. Her forbidden snack was referred to only as "fruit." While we're busting myths, Sir Isaac Newton's manuscript on gravitational theory only mentions that he observed an apple fall from a tree in his mother's garden in Lincolnshire, England. There is no evidence that the fruit ever hit him on the head.

have inspired his theory of gravity. In the case of Thomas an apple offered a remembrance of someone departed.

"We had some fruit sitting in the bottom of a deep bowl with maybe five inches between the top of the fruit and the top edge of the bowl," Thomas said. "It was two days after my mother's funeral, and suddenly one of the apples popped out of the bowl, rolled off the table, and went onto the floor."

While he couldn't be sure it was a sign from his mother Mary, Thomas found it unlikely that the fruit jumped out of the bowl on its own.

The Siren of Slocum

Music stirs deep and primitive emotions in the human psyche. It can evoke the joy of celebrations, the sadness of loss, and in the case of one innocent, summer fishing trip Thomas took with his son, the fear of the otherworldly.

Thomas's father, Leonard, was a retired coal miner born in the early 1900s in the Nanticoke area of Pennsylvania. He was a very tough man—so tough that when he was in his nineties and broke his hip, he walked several blocks to the hospital by himself for treatment. That was all the more remarkable when you consider that he suffered from emphysema and black lung disease.

How old were you when you had your first psychic experience?

"I was thirty-five. My wife and I both saw it happen so we told other people, about it. An apple jumped right out of a bowl by itself. We just looked at each other. We didn't know what to think."

—Thomas

Leonard lived independently until he was in his midnineties. He then became sick for a brief time, before passing away.

"About a week or two after my father died, I took my son Thomas Jr. to Mud Pond in Slocum, Pennsylvania, for some fishing," Thomas said. Mud Pond is atop a mountain about fifteen miles southwest of Wilkes-Barre. In the 1990s it was a nearly deserted area, providing a private haven in which Thomas and Thomas Jr. could fish for bass.

"We heard this female voice singing a church song," he recalled. "It kept going on and on for maybe ten to twelve minutes in the woods. But nobody was there. It was a scary, eerie type of sound.

"That scared my son. He didn't want to fish after that. He wanted to go home." Thomas Jr. was nine years old at the time. Thomas can't recall if they caught any fish that day, but the sound of the disembodied woman singing remains etched into his memory.

Connie and Leo

Connie and Leo were not particularly psychic. But like me, they found themselves surrounded by people who were. They married in June 1960, and ten months later, they had a honeymoon baby. Connie had hoped for a girl and planned to name her Stephanie. When a boy arrived instead, the name was converted to Stephen. Their son turned out to have inherited a rich vein of psychic ability from his grandmother Dolores. The following three chapters describe more than four decades of his psychic experiences.

Introducing the newly married couple Connie and Leo, Stephen's parents.

CHAPTER 2:

WALKING AMID ETHER AND GHOSTS

At four years old, I disrupted our church services by announcing to our minister that in one year he would not be around anymore.
—Irene Hughes, American psychic (1920–2012)

Stephen takes a spin in a carnival ride at the Jersey Shore.

Earliest Memories

Many children fantasize about riding on a flying carpet; not too many accurately simulate the experience.

Stephen grew up in a three-story home built in 1917 in Belleville, New Jersey, a historic town bordering Newark. Belleville was first settled in the 1700s, officially becoming a township in 1839. The town is best known as the birthplace of Frankie Valli and the Four Seasons. History buffs might also recognize it as the first place a steam engine was used in the United States. During the 1960s, this urban satellite of New York City was inhabited by working-class families, most of whom were close-knit, first-generation Americans.

Stephen's house, like most others in his neighborhood, had plaster walls, large, arching doorways, and thick oaken woodwork throughout. Homes in Belleville were crowded together with barely a car width between them, sometimes less. A chain-link fence surrounded the twenty or so feet of grassy backyard where Stephen (pollen allowing) and his two younger brothers played with their GI Joe action figures.

How old were you when you had your first psychic experience?

"I was aware of my psychic ability at about age fourteen. I'd had experiences before that but didn't understand what they were."

—Stephen

My future husband's bedroom was on the second floor, beneath the floor that, in previous times, would have been the servants' quarters. With three boys to raise, his mother, Connie, was as strict as a drill sergeant but loving and protective. His father, a salesman, worked long hours and was frequently on the road. Often Stephen and his brothers were in bed by the time their father returned home.

As a typical Catholic boy, Stephen didn't know much outside of catechism regarding the spiritual world. True, his family had many members possessing a sixth sense, but he had never heard about more esoteric experiences, such as out-of-body travel. So at age eight, when he began having what he innocently referred to as "pillow dreams," he had no idea what was truly going on.

Stephen was occasionally given hay-fever medicine that made him drowsy. Lulled into a hypnotic state, he found himself riding on his bedroom pillow like Aladdin on his magic carpet. He soared above his home, gliding over rooftops, busy streets, a nearby bridge spanning the Passaic River, and the steeple of an old church in the neighboring town of Kearny toward his aunt Anna's home.

Somehow he never quite reached his destination, but the aerial view of the surrounding area was something he saw repeatedly, providing a geographic observation of northern New Jersey that few people saw in the days before Google Earth. Later, these memories would prove useful to him when he rode his bicycle around Belleville and nearby towns. He never got lost.

Invisible Mall Rat

Window-shopping can be an enjoyable activity, but most people browse with their feet firmly planted on the pavement. It was not always so with Stephen.

One September evening in 1977, when Stephen was sixteen, he dozed off in his room and stepped out of his body. He found himself floating from above urban Belleville, with its tangle of highways and wall-to-wall buildings, to an area of New Jersey where rooftops spread out like islands amid a sea of lush trees. By now out-of-body travel was a familiar concept to him, so he didn't give this mystical mode of transport any more thought than getting into his parents' car for a short trip. He arrived twenty miles away at the Rockaway Townsquare Mall in Rockaway, New Jersey, just before its grand opening. Stephen walked around inside, taking his own personal, astral tour.

"The lights were off and the gates were down in all the stores," he recalled. "But the shelves were stocked and ready to go. I went into the Waldenbooks store and saw three *New Avengers* paperbacks that I wanted to read." He continued to check out all the new stores. After an evening of browsing, he returned to his body still resting back at home.

The following week his father announced that he was taking the family to a new shopping center. Stephen had never heard of Rockaway before, but when his father pulled into the parking lot, he immediately recognized the mall as the place he had visited during his out-of-body adventure the week before. As they walked through the main entrance, he spotted the Waldenbooks store and went inside with his mother. He knew which shelf the books he sought were on, but he couldn't immediately find them because someone had piled other books in front of them. He pulled the obstructing books aside to reveal the *New Avengers* series he had seen during his astral tour, and then he bought them.

Afterward Stephen told his mother that he wanted to look at the other bookstores and would meet her later in the center court of the mall, in an area that could not be seen from where they were standing.

She agreed to look for the center court and meet him there but first asked, "How do you know where everything is? We've never been here before."

"Yes, I've been here before," he replied. "You're just not going to believe how." Stephen then described his out-of-body experience to his mother. While many mothers would have been skeptical, she'd grown up with a mother who had psychic ability, and she quickly understood his experience.

Out-of-Body Excursions

The basic premise behind out-of-body (OBE) travel is this: We are souls who happen to be contained inside of a body that allows us to get around in the physical world. Sometimes our souls can leave the body for a short while and wander around a bit. The term "out-of-body experience" was actually coined in 1943 by George N. M. Tyrrell in his book *Apparitions*. Another popular term for this phenomenon is astral projection. By no means confined to the twentieth century, OBEs were part of many ancient religious traditions, including Hindu and Egyptian teachings. Written accounts of OBEs from ancient Egypt describe the experience as a sensation of traveling down a tunnel, with wind rushing in one's ears and a strange feeling of vibrations.

Snubbed by the Light

Adolescence is not an easy period for most people, and Stephen was no exception. He kept a journal tucked in his bed between the mattress and box spring, which chronicled his deepening depression. He had rarely been able to spend time outside or get involved in sports because of his allergies, so he had little in common with the other boys in his neighborhood.

It was the late 1970s. Jimmy Carter was president, following President Richard Nixon, who had resigned halfway through his second term due to the Watergate scandal. The communal altruistic sixties had faded into the self-absorbed seventies, favoring self-interest over the quest for a better world and leaving many people of all ages feeling emotionally stranded.

Early one morning Stephen was up in his room by himself when he decided to leave his body for good. If he could take small astral trips at will, he reasoned, then why not check out altogether? He lay down on his bed and drifted off, determined not to wake up. He left his body as he had done so many times before, but this time he experienced the sensation of moving down a long, black corridor in a state of anxiety.

"As I traveled farther along, the tunnel lightened in color from dark gray to light gray to white," he recalled. "I noticed that my anxiety melted away and was replaced by a feeling of peace." At the end of the tunnel, Stephen saw the wavy figures of people reaching out toward him. "I tried to reach back. Wherever I was, there was no more fear or depression. It felt like home." He knew that this was where he *wanted* to be, but soon he found out that this was not where he was *supposed* to be.

Suddenly he heard his mother's voice, snapping him back into his body like an elastic band, jolting him wide awake. She was calling him from downstairs.

She said, "I've been calling you for about an hour and a half. Where have you been?" That was a difficult question for Stephen to answer. His body had been lying in bed, but his soul had been someplace else.

Unknowingly, Stephen had opened a door when he had taken that trip down the tunnel. After his self-imposed, near-death episode, a new chapter of experiences kicked in that went well beyond his previous out-of-body journeys.

Did you react to your first psychic experience by sharing it with others or keeping it to yourself?

"At first the only one who knew was my mom. It reminded her of her mother, Grandma Dolores, who was psychic. I thought it was cool. To travel to another place that I didn't even know about was pretty amazing."
—Stephen

Death Watch

One common problem psychics have is not knowing how much of their knowledge comes psychically versus from conversations or reading. As a result, they can sometimes stun others with what they say, because they will talk about situations that are clearly beyond their experience.

Stephen's first job at age eighteen was as a graphic artist and typesetter for a small business located within walking distance of his house. One Monday morning, as he was taking his coat off at his desk, his supervisor came by to share some sad news. A female coworker, Marie, would not be in that day because her husband, John, had died on Friday. Without thinking, Stephen looked up at his boss and replied, "Oh, yes, it must have been difficult for her when she walked in the door and found him dead in the rocking chair in front of the fireplace."

After a moment of silence, his supervisor, taken aback, asked him, "How did you know that?"

Another pause filled the space between them. At first Stephen wasn't sure how he knew. Then it came back to him. Hearing about John's death had triggered a dormant memory. Stephen had gone home on Friday, and after a long day of work, he had decided to start his weekend off with a nap. When Marie's husband was dying, Stephen in his sleep state could hear John call out for someone. Marie had not yet arrived home from work, and somehow Stephen was drawn to the scene.

John was resting in his living room. The fireplace was ablaze, flickering soft shadows around him as he sat in his rocking chair. From the astral plane Stephen watched over him as he closed his eyes and peacefully passed away.

Time Slipping

"Time slipping is the ultimate déjà vu," Stephen said. It's a phenomenon in which a person somehow travels into the future for a brief period of time. One might see the next day's headlines or something else that does not yet exist in the present. In Stephen's case his time slipping involved seeing completed drafting assignments before he had drawn them.

"One day my supervisor came in with an assignment to draw a container ship with a map showing where on the deck each container should be placed," Stephen said. "Before he had a chance to explain the job, I jumped in and said, 'Oh, I know how to do this. We've done it before.'" Then Stephen proceeded to explain in detail how the assignment should be done.

His supervisor looked at him, perplexed, and said, "This is a new client. We've never done this before. But what you've described was the direction that I was given."

In Stephen's mind he was taking the assignment and doing it for the second time. For three weeks, with every assignment he was given, he ended up having to "redo" the job in a similar fashion.

"That made my work much easier," he quipped.

Workaholic Ghost

Being a workaholic is not a healthy way of life. It's also not the best way to spend one's afterlife. But even misguided ghosts can be encouraged to move on to something better.

During the 1970s and 1980s, almost everyone in northern New Jersey worked for AT&T or had a relative who did. Stephen worked for the company as a long-term temporary employee and commuted every day to a glass-enclosed corporate building in Parsippany, New Jersey. The graphic arts department where he worked had desks in a big, open room.

That room had a strange history.

Before he had joined the department, an employee there died in a bizarre mishap. As the story goes, she had visited a psychic as a joke. When she asked the psychic what her future would be, she was told that she had no future. Frightened, she ran out of the building and was hit and killed by a truck. This sounds suspiciously like an urban legend, but in this particular case it actually happened. (It's worth noting that no responsible professional psychic would ever tell someone they had no future. They tend to be careful about not causing emotional harm to those who consult them. Also, predictions may be wrong.)

Anyone who sat in the deceased employee's seat after that macabre event experienced health problems. One woman suffered a stroke on the way to work. Another employee ended up in the hospital with fibrous tumors. The seemingly cursed seat was finally given to Stephen.

He soon sensed a presence there. His coworkers told him that the woman who died had been rather paranoid. She used to leave

17

a tape recorder running after she left work so she could hear what conversations took place in her absence. Her life revolved obsessively around her job.

Based on the tales he had heard and the energy he sensed, Stephen grew to believe that the same combination of paranoia and dedication to work might have contributed to the deceased woman haunting her old desk.

"You could sense she was there," he said.

He recalled one incident that occurred when he and a coworker, Debbie, were working late into the night on a project. They spent hours in a special camera room to process fifty photostats, a now-obsolete way that illustrations were reproduced so they could be cut and pasted down on layouts for printing.

After they finished processing the photostats, Stephen and Debbie pinned them on the wall to dry with pushpins. Then they went back to their desks to work on other things. When they returned to the photostat room a half hour later, they made a shocking discovery. All of the now-dry photostats had been removed from the wall and neatly stacked on a nearby desk. Stunned, Stephen and Debbie looked at each other.

"It was three in the morning. We both knew that no one else had gone in or out of the photostat room—except, perhaps, a ghostly workaholic," Stephen said.

They took the self-stacking photostats back to their desks to complete the project, and Stephen thanked the ghost employee for her help.

"I think she was happy to know that someone could understand her," he said.

The woman's ghost seemed to confine herself to the second floor, where the art department and main offices were located. Another ghost appeared to inhabit the third floor. Stephen frequented a deserted area of the building on the third floor late at night to think. It had a dark, quiet atmosphere that he found peaceful. To access it he had to walk down an internal windowless hallway.

"Late one night I saw a ball of light traveling down the hallway in front of me with the same sort of bounce and pace you might see if someone were walking," he said. He pursued the orb down the hallway and around several corners for about forty feet. It went into a room, but when Stephen opened the door to follow it, it was gone.

Back on the second floor, Stephen never experienced any health problems like those that had plagued his coworkers while sitting in the dead employee's seat. He believes the ghost never hurt him because she knew he posed no threat to her and he treated her kindly. Stephen often spoke to her.

One day he thanked the ghost for her help and suggested that she didn't need to be there anymore; it was time to go home. After that he felt she eventually left. The next person who sat in her seat after Stephen didn't suffer from any health problems.

Dead Reckoning

Why do souls wander around in the physical world when they could cross over into the white light and enjoy the bliss of the afterlife? Spiritualist and author Gary Leon Hill suggests that when people die through accidents or violence, while clouded by alcohol or drugs, or simply without knowing what to expect following death, they may not realize they have died. Psychic medium George Anderson agrees. In his book *Lessons from the Light*, he says that it may take the dead a while to figure out what's happened to them in these circumstances, because the transition from life to death may be barely noticeable. On the other hand, if someone has been suffering with a terminal illness, they not only know they've died, but freed from their pain-ridden bodies, they are happy about it.

CHApteR 3

Journeys Through Souls and Time

Figuring out our gifts in life is part of our journey to becoming enlightened human beings.
            —Allison DuBois, American psychic medium (1972–)

Three psychics in a row: (l to r) young Stephen at a social occasion with his aunt Anna and grandma Dolores.

A Door Opens

There are two types of people in this world: people who like to collect things and people who like to throw things out. Stephen belongs to the former. From the time he was a teenager, he collected comic books.

"Because I worked such long hours, comics were about the only pastime I had for recreation," he said.

One Sunday back in 1988, he went to a comic book show and met a woman named Angie. She was tall and thin with playful hazel eyes, a bright orange pixie haircut, and a killer sense of humor. They hit it off and began hanging out together.

"One day I went to pick her up for a date and found that her landlady Natalie was a psychic," he recalled. Angie was late coming home from work, so Natalie invited Stephen to sit in on the psychic development class she was leading that night. He recalled the students were given two exercises.

"They took an object you owned and hid it, and you had to see if you could find it by zeroing in on your own energy," Stephen recalled. "They took my house key, and I had to find it. Otherwise, I wouldn't be able to get into my house." He walked from room to room inside the psychic's home in search of the key, tuned into his own energy, and followed it outside, where he found the key under some bushes.

Afterward the psychic asked if anyone had ever experienced astral projection, another term for out-of-body travel. Stephen was the only one in the room who had. Class members asked him to explain his experiences. The psychic then paired off participants and told them to leave their bodies and meet halfway in midair.

Stephen was paired with a young woman. He went into a meditative state, left his body, and saw her leave her body, panic, and jump back. Of all the students, he was the only one who accomplished the task.

That began Stephen's "formal" psychic education. He attended the psychic development class every Wednesday night for the next seven years.

"We studied everything in that class. We explored psychometry, which is holding any type of object belonging to someone and getting information about that person from it. This is a technique often used by psychics to find lost people. We practiced past-life regression. We used psychic kinesis to bend metal. We played with ghosts. We did shamanic journeys. It was a fascinating time."

Stephen was delighted to have found a peer group who understood his experiences and didn't find them at all strange. This was an environment where he could learn and grow.

The Messenger

It must be puzzling to deliver an important message to someone and not be privy to what you said. That can happen when someone channels information.

Channeling occurs when a person becomes a conduit for a spirit to speak directly to the living. One of the lessons Stephen learned in the class was how to give psychic readings. He soon realized that when he was performing readings, he was often channeling or taking shamanic journeys with animal guides.

Stephen's technique for reading was to hold his palms up and have his subject place his or her fingertips on his hands.

"While connecting with the person I was reading, it felt like someone was tapping me on my shoulder, and then I stood off to the side while the spirit used my body to speak." Stephen could watch what was going on and see his mouth moving, but he wasn't able to hear any of his words, so he had no idea what he was telling the person receiving the reading. Occasionally he would step out of himself completely and enter a void with no knowledge of what was going on.

One summer evening back in the late 1980s, Stephen performed a reading for a young woman. He received the familiar ghostly tap on the shoulder and stepped out of his body while a spirit stepped in.

"She was a pretty woman. I didn't know who she was. When the reading was over and I returned, she was crying," he said. "I had no idea what she had been told. Eventually, I found out a friend of hers had been murdered and the reading had gone into that, but I never found out the details."

Another time Stephen worked at a psychic fair. A thin, blonde woman in her thirties asked him for a reading about her marriage.

"She seemed very sweet," he said. "Whatever I told her, she thanked me for my advice and said she was going to give it a try. A few weeks later I received a card from her, thanking me for saving her marriage." Though it was nice to know he had helped her, Stephen never found out what he said that remedied her situation.

Channeling Through Time

Channeling is one way the dead communicate with the living. It's when spirits tap psychics on the shoulder and ask permission to deliver messages to the living through them. Ancient Egypt offers the earliest accounts of channeling through trances, but the practice was by no means confined to that region. College professor and author Jon Klimo, PhD, writes that records show the ancient Chinese, Indians, and Tibetans partook in this mystical practice thousands of years ago, and their scribes were said to have produced literature this way, including Taoist writings, the Buddhist *Tibetan Book of the Dead*, and the early Hindu *Vedas*. Essentially, the information was "dictated" to them, and they took it down.

Inner Journeys

Embarking on an excursion into the mind of another human being can be a fascinating adventure. That's what takes place when a psychic takes a shamanic journey. Essentially, the psychic travels alongside of, or merges with, a spirit guide and ventures into the mind of another to offer insights. Occasionally, a journey is made without a guide. Stephen's main spirit guide is an eagle.

"I'll become the eagle and soar until I reach a cliff face that is my private sanctuary," he said. He starts many journeys from there. Once he reaches that summit and mentally prepares himself for his travel, he adopts another animal guide such as a horse, unicorn, or tiger. "You get whatever guide can help you for the journey," he said.

In a reading for a man named Thom, Stephen found himself transported inside a cavern with walls everywhere. He was riding a horse as his spirit guide and wearing a knight's armor with a white surcoat.

"I had a sword, and I kept slamming it against the wall, eventually breaking through," he said. He continued smashing through several walls, going deeper and deeper.

"All feeling of my physical self disappeared, and I began to assume the feelings of the man I was reading," he said. These feelings included defensiveness, fear, and sadness.

Finally Stephen reached a massive cavern with a raised platform. Resting on that platform was a room with a door. In front of the door lay a sleeping dragon. Stephen dismounted from the spirit-guide horse and crept past the dragon, careful not to wake it. He pushed the door and it opened.

An all-white room met his eyes. Thom was present, sitting in a rocking chair. The wall was covered with hundreds of pictures of his son. He sat, rocking back and forth, looking around, unaware Stephen was there. Stephen stood and watched him for a while, but finally he turned around and left the man in his own world. He found himself instantaneously transported back beyond the outermost wall.

"I later found out that Thom's son had died," Stephen explained. "It was a suicide." He had felt Thom's sorrow and witnessed how it obsessed his tortured thoughts.

Ice Castles

One of the greatest challenges in shamanic journeys is achieving a reading for someone who is a very private person. While someone may consciously volunteer to have a psychic enter their mind, their unconscious self often can have a different opinion altogether.

During another exercise in his psychic development class, Stephen read for a quiet, shy woman. "She was a very sweet, innocent-looking girl with medium-length brown hair, about five feet five and a bit fleshy in build," he said. "We were sitting there. I took her hands. The next thing you know, I was in this incredible ice cavern. The walls were ice. Everything was ice. There was a flowing river that led to a lake. I walked down stairs lined with icy stalactites and stalagmites. At the bottom of the stairs was a small rowboat made of wood.

"I got in and ventured out into the lake. It was a vast body of calm water. When I rowed out far enough, this incredible ice castle, about

When you discovered your psychic ability, how did it alter the way you thought about the world around you?

"I just knew that there was something else out there past this world. And I thought, 'If I could do that, maybe I could do other things.' And things started happening."
—Stephen

forty or fifty feet high, rose into view. Surrounding the castle was a ledge, and I moored the boat to it. I stood there, analyzing the fortress, looking for a way in. The walls were sheer. There were no doors. I kept walking all the way around it, trying to figure out a way to get in." He finally decided that because it was made of ice, he could chip away at it and make footholds to climb up the wall.

"I remember looking down as I was climbing and realizing that I was up pretty high. Finally, I climbed over the ramparts and into the castle. I wound my way down the stairs into its interior. As I came down, she was there, alone, sitting on an ice throne."

He stood there, watching her for a while. Suddenly, the girl realized Stephen had entered her domain, and she lost no time transporting him back outside the wall. The castle grew higher. She was a very private person and did not want anyone inside her mind.

"I think she was kind of surprised I got in," he added. "There was nothing I could do, so I got back into the boat and returned to reality. If you have to go through this kind of battle, you know the person you're reading is not going to let you in."

The Envelope, Please

Psychometry is an area of psychic ability that has been used by some police departments to locate missing people. As mentioned previously, this skill involves holding an object belonging to someone else and getting information about that person from it. Everything we own, so the theory goes, is imbued with our energy.

In one class Stephen was trained in how to perform psychometry with some simple exercises. He was given sealed envelopes containing photos and instructed to hold each between his two palms to sense what images or feelings they evoked.

"The first one I held gave me a feeling of darkness, cold, and disconnection," he said. "The longer I held it, the more I felt something was not right, that the person was no longer there." When the envelope was opened, he found out it was a picture of someone who had died in the 1940s.

The second envelope communicated images of forests, and he saw a log cabin and horses.

"I got the feeling of a medicine woman living in the woods," he recalled. It turned out that the photo was of a woman who was a trained homeopathic healer. She lived in a wooded area and kept horses there.

Psychometry Vibes

Psychometry literally means "soul measuring." The late author and metaphysical teacher Ted Andrews described psychometry as the ability to receive impressions about past events or feelings from objects, people, or places. If one person has owned something such as clothes or jewelry, his or her imprint can be easy to discern. If an object is older, it may have been touched by many people, offering a group impression rather than a single experience. In the absence of an object, photographs can be used.

River of Molasses

It's not always easy for psychics to understand the symbols they receive in readings. Sometimes the true meaning isn't revealed until days, weeks, or years afterward.

A dark-haired woman in her midtwenties once asked Stephen to perform a reading for her. She wanted to know what her future would hold; she hoped to be a journalist.

"She had a nice smile. She was very playful, very full of life," he said. "I remember she had short hair and a tough appearance."

Stephen held her hands and concentrated. He saw mountains in upheaval, bursting up out of the ground wherever he turned. He was a bit puzzled at the repeated visions of the mountains, but they eventually gave way to other images.

"I saw a river, and it was made of molasses," he said. "On the other side of the river were three wood-paneled doors. It was a struggle to wade across the river and reach the doors. When I finally did, I found that each one I tried was locked." He wasn't sure what to tell the woman.

"I told her, 'Maybe there's a different path for you. Maybe journalism isn't what you're going to go into.'" She replied that she had always thought that journalism was what she would pursue. "I said, 'Well, things change.'"

A few weeks later he learned that she had died on a mountain while ice climbing. She had slipped and gotten trapped in a crevasse. Rescuers couldn't get to her in time, and she froze to death. That sad news affirmed in Stephen's mind the significance of the mountains and the reason why none of the doors would open. She had no future.

Waiting for a Lifetime

Why do people develop strong interests in a particular person or career? Sometimes the answer lies not in this life but in a previous one.

"Once I did a reading for a tall, thin man in his late thirties who was training to be a nurse," Stephen said. The man wasn't sure why he felt compelled to pursue nursing and asked about it for his reading.

"He came to the reading wearing green scrubs," Stephen recalled. "I thought it was going to be a typical reading, but it ended up becoming a past-life regression." They sat in darkness with only candles lighting the room. Stephen took his hands and tried to delve into why nursing was in the man's life.

"Next thing I knew, I was hearing cannon fire, gunshots, and screaming. I opened up my third eye and found we were near a battlefield. I was hearing the sounds of men fighting, screaming, and dying. We were in a home that had been commandeered to provide a makeshift hospital. I began moving around and found we were in Vicksburg, Mississippi, on a hot spring or summer day. It was the Battle of Vicksburg during the Civil War.

"The longer I stayed in the area, the more real everything started to become. I could begin smelling the cordite from the discharge of the muskets and the freshness of the grass. I could feel the hard ground underneath me. The screams of the men became louder. Even though we were not on the actual battlefield, I could feel the awful percussion of the cannons. I found myself walking around this field hospital. I could smell rotting flesh and saw piles of rotting limbs. It was horrible.

"I saw that the nursing student was a field doctor there. He was running around, taking care of the wounded and dying, feeling frustrated at not being able to save lives and limbs."

Stephen described the scene to the man, who replied that now it made sense to him why he was going into the medical field. The technology finally existed for him to truly help his patients.

Reincarnation
Reincarnation refers to the belief that when we die, our souls eventually are reborn into another body to live again. The physical world is a classroom in which we learn lessons to help our souls evolve. Eventually, when we have learned everything we need to know, we no longer return. In her book *Reincarnation: The Missing Link in Christianity*, Elizabeth Clare Prophet estimates that over one-fifth of American adults believe in reincarnation. Reincarnation has been a cornerstone of many religions for thousands of years in Tibet, India, ancient Egypt, and ancient Greece. It was carried over into early Christianity but declared heresy in 533 AD by the Council of Constantinople.

Out of Egypt

Just as some people like to wander on vacations without any particular itinerary or purpose, some psychic readings provide a glimpse of something interesting with no readily discernible lesson or meaning. It's an interesting journey, and that's about it.

One summer evening in the early 1990s, Stephen performed a reading for a man who had no particular questions. Sometimes people are not looking for insights on any specific situation in their lives; they just want a reading for the experience. After taking the man's hands, Stephen asked permission to go into his subconscious and found himself riding on a conveyer belt into his subject's mind. Immediately he felt heat on his back and roughness on his hands, and then he began physically leaning over.

"I could feel gravel or sand under my feet. It was shifting under me. My feet were either bare or lightly covered. I wasn't sure what was going on around me. I opened my third eye to find out where I was and what was happening. Next thing I knew, I looked up and saw a pyramid block in front of me. There were no whips, guards, or chains. I was not pushing this block under duress. I was working with thousands of other men on this because I wanted to. The longer I stayed there, the more real it became. I could feel the hot sand beneath my feet, the coarseness of the stone, and the heat of the day. I realized that I was not a slave. I was a worker. I don't know why those images came up. The images surprised the man I was reading as well."

Finally, the vision ended. "We never knew why it emerged. Sometimes you don't know why you see something or what it means."

Fatal Recall

At one time or another most people have had the experience of meeting an individual who appeared perfectly nice, but who, for some reason, set off internal alarm bells. Is this a warning that should be heeded, or is something else more complex at work?

In the late 1980s, Stephen had a freelance job as a graphic artist at a small manufacturing company, drawing packaging for car-part products.

"It was a friendly environment," he said. "My supervisor introduced me to everyone in the department. Most of the people I met had good energy." One man, however, had a strange effect on him when they shook hands.

"I suddenly got a sharp, jabbing pain in my chest," Stephen recalled. "The weird thing was, whenever I ran into him, I experienced the same pain all over again." Naturally, Stephen began to avoid the man in any way he could.

In one of his psychic development classes, Stephen's teacher told him that the man who caused his chest pains had probably killed him in a previous life. Stephen was given a past-life regression, and he began to see that lifetime.

"I had been a spice trader in Hong Kong, married with a daughter," Stephen recalled. "On one of my voyages, my ship was attacked by pirates and the cargo was stolen. I saw my own death as he stabbed me straight through the chest with a sword. Then I watched my ship burning and sinking."

Afterward Stephen's teacher told him he needed to forgive the man.

The next day at work Stephen concentrated on forgiveness. It seemed to work, because after that he no longer experienced the pain. Their past-life karma was settled.

The Spinning Rack

The dead often try to communicate with people they sense are able to perceive them. But when they are confused and lost, they may have no apparent purpose other than letting others know they exist.

After Stephen's time as a freelance graphic artist, he decided to take a job as the manager of a comic book shop in Boonton, New Jersey. The store was located in a very old building on Main Street. In the front of the store, there was a spinning rack for comics. Due to the angle of the old, uneven wood floor, the rack was weighted so that it could only spin in one direction. The back of the store had shallow-ledge shelving that also held comics. A protective lip held them face out and kept them from sliding off if someone brushed by.

One humid summer evening at the store, Stephen chatted with a customer and friend, David, who was also psychic. It was a slow night and he was glad for the company. Both of them were sweltering in the ninety-degree heat because the store didn't have air conditioning.

"Suddenly we noticed that the rack by the front door began to spin in the opposite direction than it was weighted," he said. Then they watched as the magazines at the back of the store began to flip up over the shelf ledges onto the floor, one by one, from left to right.

Stephen's focus immediately locked in on the expensive comics flying off the shelf, and he yelled, "Stop it!" It stopped about two-thirds of the way down the row. David, being a paranormal investigator, walked slowly around the store, trying to sense the origin of the disturbance.

"He detected a cold spot in one section of the store," Stephen said. "It was quite noticeable because the rest of the store was so very hot and humid."

After Stephen reshelved all of the fallen comics, he went to the spot David pointed out, and he could also feel the cold. He stood there for a time and tried to measure out the cold space.

"It was about a two-foot area," Stephen said. He went into the basement and, standing in the same spot one floor below, could still feel the cold spot.

"It was a vertical disturbance in the area that went through both floors of the building," he said.

He returned upstairs, walked into the cold spot, and held his hands out with palms facing downward to feel the energy.

"I waited and it got colder, the type of cold where you could see your breath," he said. "Then I heard a little girl crying."

The longer he stayed in that spot, the more audible her crying became. David stood in the cold spot and also heard the little girl. She had passed away long ago, but for some reason she was stuck there.

When David moved out of the cold area, he became temporarily blind. Stephen guided him over to a chair so he could sit and regain his vision. About an hour later David's sight returned.

The men couldn't figure out why the little girl was crying or why she didn't move on. Her visitation left more questions than answers, because after that hot evening, her troubled spirit never returned.

Soul Peer Groups

Souls reincarnate in peer groups, according to research done by Michael Newton, PhD. He hypnotized numerous people to discover what they did between lifetimes and published his results in *Journey of Souls*. Newton writes that one's closest relatives and friends are likely to be a part of their soul peer group. Together they embark on learning adventures over many lifetimes and are bonded for eternity. Perhaps we unconsciously recognize our spirit clique, and this is why certain people we encounter in life effortlessly become close friends.

The Gateway

Meditation has often been described as a gateway to spirituality, and it is part of the religious tradition in many countries. In Western culture it is a common technique for achieving a sense of personal peace.

Stephen has meditated at various periods in his life, but the most memorable spiritual experience he had was in Cancun, Mexico, in 1988. A full moon shimmered on the ocean. Near midnight he sat on the beach, facing the lapping waves, closed his eyes, and cleared his mind.

"Gradually, I felt myself melting into everything around me," he said. "I was the waves gently rippling on the beach, the birds circling in the skies above, the fish moving in the waters, and the dolphins swimming near the shoreline. I was one with everything." He achieved a state of euphoria for the first time.

Outside of his body Stephen could see himself sitting on the beach.

"I was all and nothing at the same time. It was the ultimate getting rid of who you think you are and being everything," he recalled. This experience occurred during a transitional period in his life when he was coming into his own spirituality.

"I didn't quite understand what was happening to me. These things just unfolded." He believes the meditative experience was a shedding of old injuries and a delving down into who he really was.

The beach in Cancun where Stephen meditated.

Meditation Through Time

Meditation may well have been practiced long before recorded history, beginning with early hunters and gatherers staring into hypnotic campfires. It's thought that meditative practices likely originated in India, where they are mentioned in the oldest recorded literature, the *Ṛg Veda*, composed between 1500–1000 BC. Taoist literature in China describes well-defined meditation practices as early as 300 BC. Socrates's biography also mentions his achieving ecstasy through meditation. Willard Johnson, in his book *Riding the Ox Home: A History of Meditation from Shamanism to Science,* suggests that Moses, Plato, Christ, and Muhammad used ecstatic meditative states to achieve their profound philosophical and spiritual insights.

Letting Go

When a loved one passes, letting go is an important part of the grieving process, not only with friends and family but also with beloved pets.

Stephen was "owned" by two cats when he was growing up. One was a tortoiseshell calico named Tiger and the other was her son, a black tuxedo cat named Blackie. Toward the end of Tiger's life, she developed peritonitis. She became very weak and would sometimes suddenly stop and fall over.

"There were a number of times when Mom and I thought Tiger had died, but she would get up again and walk away," Stephen said. One night Tiger dropped in front of Stephen, and suddenly he could read her mind.

"I'm not comfortable," she said. "I want to die, but I can't while people are in the house. I have to die alone."

"It felt like we were holding her back from leaving," Stephen said. "She really did want to go." On a morning soon after, before he left for work, he saw Tiger standing by the stairs. "I looked at her and I said good-bye."

Sometime that afternoon he received a panicked phone call from his mother. She had found Tiger sprawled dead in her bedroom. It was

Memorial Day weekend. No veterinarians were open, so his parents weren't sure what to do with her. Finally, they found a pet hospital that would take her body. His mother was in a state of panic about leaving Tiger behind. She had never had a pet when she was younger, so this was her first experience with losing a beloved animal.

"A day or so later I was in the bathroom getting ready for work," Stephen said. "I thought I saw a shadow coming into the room. When I turned around, Tiger was sitting on the hamper in full corporeal [solid] form. So I looked at her and said, 'You're not happy, are you?'" Then the cat faded away.

His mother, at times, could sense Tiger's presence curling up in her lap. Tiger hung around for a couple of days before Stephen finally realized the problem.

"I told Mom, 'You're holding on to her. You have to let go.'" That night his mother dreamt that she saw Tiger standing in the front foyer. Tiger jumped into her arms then turned into human form and told her, "You have to let me go. I'm not happy here."

"Mom understood. She put her down. The cat turned back to her feline form and went away." After that they no longer sensed the cat in the house. She had crossed over and was at peace.

In addition to saying good-bye to Tiger, Stephen's family also lost Blackie, Tiger's son, several months later.

"Blackie died of a broken heart," Stephen said. "He didn't want to live without his mother."

Both cats had been part of the family since Stephen was a teenager. Now he was thirty years old. With his faithful companions gone, he felt this was the beginning of a new phase in his life. Stephen had spent most of his twenties buried in his work and in psychic development classes. A romantic, he found himself wishing that he would finally meet the woman he would marry. He was lonely and it was time. It's said that when we ask for something from the heart, the universe hears our requests. Stephen's wish was answered within a month after Blackie's departure, as you'll see in the next chapter.

Pets Crossing Over
More than 60 percent of all households in this country have a pet, according to the American Society for the Prevention of Cruelty to Animals. We love them dearly, but as all pet owners know, eventually we have to say good-bye. In her book *All Pets Go to Heaven*, psychic medium Sylvia Browne writes that all pets immediately cross over to the light after they die. Sometimes they come back and visit, and when they do, their owners can often sense them brushing against their legs or hopping onto their beds. When humans cross over, says George Anderson in his book *Lessons from the Light*, their pets are often the first to greet them, because their loving and nonjudgmental presence makes the transition easier.

CHAPTER 4

THE PSYCHIC HANDSHAKE AND UNSEEN WORLDS

The minute I heard my first love story, I started looking for you, not knowing how blind that was. Lovers don't finally meet somewhere—they are in each other all along.

—Rumi, Turkish Sufi mystic (1207–1273)

The Psychic Handshake

People who read energy can sense its meaning in every place they visit or person they meet. I know that sounds rather vague, but that's what I've been told. I don't sense energy, so I can only pass along how others have described it. Basically, psychics get impressions, for example, of people's personalities, good or bad intentions, or state of health. They can also feel if a place has positive or negative energy based on events that may have happened there in the past. This offers psychics the advantage or disadvantage of knowing more about people and places than those of us without such sensitivities.

Stephen and I first crossed paths in the fall of 1992. He'd been attending a psychic development class for several years. I worked as a writer and interviewed the

Stephen, trying to look thoughtful.

woman who ran those classes for an article. She invited me to attend her weekly gathering, and about a year later, I took her up on the offer, although I was admittedly a bit skeptical about psychics.

When I arrived the teacher introduced me to a group of her regular students. One somber young man, dressed in a dark suit and sporting a black fedora, shook my hand. His name was Stephen.

As Stephen tells it, when you shake someone's hand, there's usually a momentary shift in energy that, if you're sensitive to energy—which I'm not—you can feel. Apparently, everyone is enveloped by electromagnetic fields that vibrate at a unique rate. These are sometimes referred to as auras. When Stephen shook my hand, he didn't feel any shift in energy. That's because we were vibrating at the same rate—something that is quite rare. He says he knew at that moment that we were soul mates and would someday marry.

I, of course, had no idea about that. But the following year, we walked down the aisle together. That was more than twenty years ago, so I guess his intuition was right.

Vibrational Energy
Every conscious being sends or receives vibrational energy based on their thoughts, feelings, and beliefs, writes Kenneth McClean in his book *The Vibrational Universe*. Since everyone has a unique combination of thoughts, feelings, and beliefs, it may follow that we are all vibrating at our own unique rates. The term "vibrational" is also seen in the field of quantum physics, where it has been observed that all living beings (people, animals, and plants) have unique vibrational frequencies or energy fields.

Residual Fear

"A house is not an inanimate object. It has life. It has energy," Stephen said. But where does that energy originate?

For about a year before I met Stephen, I had a recurring dream that I was in an old house, searching for someone who was hiding. I went up a wide flight of stairs to a landing that led up to an attic room. I was intent on hunting for this person; I don't know if I ever found him. That was the extent of the dream. I had never seen the house in my waking moments.

When we first began dating, Stephen invited me to a Halloween party thrown by one of his friends, Trish. Trish lived in a large, historic home in Boonton, New Jersey, that had been a part of the Underground Railroad.

History buffs may recall that the Underground Railroad consisted of a network of secret routes and safe houses used by nineteenth-century black slaves in the United States to escape to free states and Canada. They did so with the aid of abolitionists, people who believed that slavery was immoral and should be abolished. The Underground Railroad reached its height in the ten years leading up to the Civil War. The Fugitive Slave Act of 1850 made it legal for federal agents to pursue escaped slaves in the North, driving many to flee to Canada, lest they be kidnapped and returned to their owners.

Many Boonton residents in the 1800s, such as Mayor and State Assemblyman Charles Hopkins, were active in transporting runaway slaves from one community to another. The house where the Halloween party was held had been an area safe house. It was a spacious structure, three stories in height, with an old-fashioned porch that wrapped around the front and sides.

Trish gave us a tour of the house. As we reached a landing going up to the top floor, Stephen and I both stopped and looked at each other.

"I've been here before," Stephen said. I had the same strong feeling.

Stephen began to describe the room upstairs before we got there. It was a large open space with walls lined with storage cabinets. One wall had windows overlooking the front yard. When we entered I knew it was the place from my recurring dreams where I had been in pursuit of someone. Stephen, on the other hand, tapped into a different experience.

"When we got up there, I had the sensation of being closed in, of hiding," Stephen said. "And I felt a tremendous fear. It was very overpowering. After a while I had to get out of there, because it was really disturbing. That's when you said something. That you had this feeling you were searching for someone."

That was also when the owner told us about the role the house had played in the Underground Railroad. I never had the dream again after our visit, and I am not sure what it meant.

"I may have been tapping into energy that was trapped in the house and in that room," Stephen said. "It was very strong, but I didn't get the feeling until I hit that landing."

Apparently, strong emotions can leave residual energy in a room long after its inhabitants are gone. It was an interesting experience for me, and an early introduction to what Stephen could read in the psychometry of a building.

A Ghost in the House

Older homes often are referred to as money pits because of the hidden problems contained within their walls. But unfinished business is not always limited to the physical aspect of a home. Other loose ends can also be lurking on the premises.

About a month before tying the knot, Stephen and I found a dilapidated house begging for tender, loving care. It required many hours of painting and light carpentry. Stephen would stop off at our house after work and carry on with renovations. His naïvely ambitious plan was to convert it to move-in condition before we married in July.

One night while he was alone in the house, painting an upstairs bedroom, Stephen sensed someone watching him. It was late, so initially he dismissed the feeling, attributing it to fatigue after a long day at work. But as the night wore on, the presence grew stronger.

"Finally, I spun around and saw a woman standing in the doorway," he said. "She wore a full-length white dress, and her dark hair was gathered atop her head in an old-fashioned upsweep." He was struck by how young and beautiful she was. She didn't look pale, and she was corporeal, so he couldn't see through her.

Stephen's sudden movement and awareness of her presence must have taken her by surprise. Her hands flew up to her open mouth, and she quickly disappeared. This would not be the last time he saw her. Characteristically, his first reaction was, "Cool, we have a ghost in the house!"

After we moved into our home-in-progress, strange things began to happen. The radio in the kitchen would turn on by itself. There might have been a logical explanation, except that the music persisted after the cord was pulled out of the socket.

The second time Stephen saw the woman was just after he'd lost his job as a graphic artist at a now-defunct local magazine. He was sitting on the couch in the living room, feeling despondent. Suddenly she materialized next to him and put her arm around his shoulders.

She said, "Don't worry. Everything is going to be fine." Then she took him back in time to visit what her life had been like and where she'd lived.

"She transported us to a small home," he said. "We walked through the rooms, and I noticed there was a blur of other people. But this was just a glimpse of the past. They were no longer there."

The woman said she used to picnic in the area where our house was now standing. In the early part of the twentieth century, she had been thrown from a moving automobile nearby and died. She told him telepathically that her name was Melissa. He recalled that she was fully corporeal the entire time.

"She was a good soul," Stephen said. "She'd just somehow been forgotten and was still wandering around the area. She was happy that our small home was occupied." She hung around the place, but she didn't bother anyone.

The final time Stephen saw Melissa was about five years later, when he was in bed. It was in the early hours of the morning.

"I woke up, opened my eyes, and saw a vortex spinning above me," he said. "It was a portal between here and the next world. It looked like a spinning black hole, and I could feel my soul being pulled away from my body." Melissa was in front of the whirling energy field and was asking Stephen to come with her since he'd been so kind.

He replied, "It's your time to go home; it's not mine." She pleaded with him to join

How has your unfolding psychic ability affected the way you treat other people, both those you know and strangers?

"I don't think it changed anything. I was always taught to be good to other people, including strangers."
—Stephen

her, but he insisted that people were waiting for *her* on the other side. It was time for *her* to go.

"It took everything I had to hold my soul in my body because of how strong the vortex was. Eventually, she began to lift up and walk toward the energy spiral. It was the bridge between here and the other side," Stephen said. She went into it, her hand still reaching out to him. Again he resisted. At last she turned and moved on into the whirling vortex. The portal closed slowly like an aperture behind her.

The entire time, I was sleeping soundly next to Stephen, unaware of what was happening. Melissa had finally crossed over to the other side. Stephen never saw her again and was glad she was now at peace.

The Deposit

When a person feels dread about an impending situation, sometimes it's best to acknowledge that feeling. It may provide a shield from trouble or even save a life.

In the mid-1990s, Stephen was an assistant manager for a carpeting store. While working a night shift, he felt uneasy; something wasn't right. As the evening progressed, he became increasingly agitated whenever he got near the money in the cash register. That was troubling, because it was his turn to close out the register at the end of the evening then drop the money off at the bank. The other assistant manager he was working with that night, Dave, asked Stephen if something was wrong; he wasn't his usual self. Normally, the two joked with each other while they worked, but that evening Stephen was very serious.

"I told him I didn't want anything to do with the deposit that night, and I asked if he could he do it for me," Stephen said. His intuition was telling him that on this night Dave was the better person to handle the task. "He said, 'Fine. No problem.' So I did the close out and gave him the money to deposit."

When they finally left the store, it was about ten thirty at night. Stephen went home and Dave set out for the bank. The bank was a few miles up the road, located in a poorly lit, deserted area. To drop off the money, the depositor had to get out of the car and, using a key and a special coded lock, put the money into a chute, which went directly into the building.

It wasn't until the following day that Stephen learned Dave was going to be late for work. That was because he was giving information to the police about an attempted robbery from the night before.

"It turned out that two men had come up and hit him from behind. Unfortunately for them, Dave was over six feet tall and built like a football player. He had previously worked as an armored-truck guard and knew how to defend himself. After they knocked him down, the thieves grabbed the money, but Dave recovered quickly, wheeled around, struck one man, and brought him to the ground. Then he chased the other man, and as the fleeing thief was trying to get into his car, Dave slammed the door onto his leg, shattering his bones." His attackers subdued, Dave deposited the money, called the police, and calmly waited for them to arrive with an ambulance. Both suspects ended up in the hospital.

Dave had no problem dispatching his assailants. But his less athletic coworker wouldn't have fared as well. The experience affirmed what Stephen had always believed: it's important to listen to your inner voice.

"If something doesn't feel right, heed it. There's generally a reason."

The Case for Premonitions

Time is a concept, but is it real? People tend to assume that the past, present, and future unfold chronologically, but no scientist has ever proven that. To the contrary, writes Larry Dossey, MD, some physicists theorize about time traveling in loops that can carry information from the future to now. Others suggest that the mind is not confined to our bodies and is infinite. If that were the case, then everyone potentially would have access to the future—*if only one could figure out how to unlock that information!*

Pushy Customer

When you work in retail, you learn to deal with pushy customers, but not the kind that Stephen encountered one day back in 2008 when he was the assistant manager for a mall bookstore.

Stephen's coworker Mary was in charge of the children's section in the back of the store.

"She came to me one time and asked if I sensed something in the store, because she knew I could perceive energy," Stephen said. Mary complained that when she was shelving books she always felt as if she were being watched. The feeling was so strong that it made her uncomfortable. But when she turned around to see who was peering over her shoulder, no one was there.

"I went back to the children's section that particular day, and I didn't sense anything," he said. "A couple of times after that I checked it out, but I still felt nothing."

Finally, one afternoon when Mary wasn't scheduled to come in, Stephen caught a glimpse of what she'd been sensing.

"I was straightening up shelves at the front of the store when I saw someone standing in the children's section," he said. "I didn't remember him coming in. So I walked to the back to see if he needed any help. Then I noticed that he wasn't there. I thought he might be on the other side of the tall shelf. When I came around the other side, I saw a grayish, shadowy figure with obscured facial features. I guess this entity must have been startled that I could see it, because it actually pushed me to the side into the shelves and ran past me down the aisle toward the front of the store. I lost my footing and fell down. When I got up, I ran to the front of the store where my supervisor was standing and asked if he'd seen anyone run by. He said no." Stephen didn't bother explaining why he'd asked; his manager didn't believe in ghosts. Nor did Stephen share the information with Mary, because he didn't want to frighten her.

"I felt him again from time to time, especially late at night," Stephen said, "but he never pushed me again."

Bad Company

For those who are sensitive to psychic energy, life can be complex.

While still working as the assistant manager of the mall bookstore, Stephen encountered a woman named Karen whose energy field had a strange effect on him. Apparently, the feeling was mutual. Whenever Karen came in to shop, they would both become sick if they stood within twenty feet of each other.

"She was a mom who came in to shop with her three small children," he recalled. "We used to laugh about it. She would come in and ask for help on finding a book, and I would shout what she needed to know from across the store at a safe distance."

One day, as he was standing by the register, Stephen's leg developed a shooting pain then went numb and gave out under him. His coworker asked what was wrong, but Stephen said he didn't know. The pain was so severe that he had to hold himself up by leaning on the counter.

"Just then, I saw Karen enter the store with a cast on her leg and crutches." The two of them had some strange physical empathy. They could never figure out why.

"She was a nice person," he said. "We just couldn't get near each other."

Spiritual Bartender

Stephen has told me he often feels like a friendly neighborhood bartender. In several places he's worked throughout his life, complete strangers would approach him and ask for advice. They would be puzzled as to why they were talking so familiarly to a stranger and would tell him so. However, for some curious reason they felt he was the one to ask.

Stephen would say whatever popped into his mind. Then, a week or so later, they would return and thank him. Whatever advice he doled out always seemed to work out for the best.

One patron said to him, "I'm not sure about a job interview I'm going to. I'm not sure if it's the right path for me." Stephen told him not to worry and to go to the

Stephen at the seasonal calendar store he managed for Borders.

interview. He did, got the job, and came back with his girlfriend to thank Stephen.

"Such is the life of a psychic bartender," said Stephen. However, he insisted that he deserved no credit; he just delivered the messages.

Fate Forward

For those who believe in predestination (that some events are fated to happen), it's said that there are many possible exit dates for a person to leave this earthly plane. When and how one dies depends upon the collective decisions oneself and others make in life.

One day in 2001 Stephen had a premonition that I would be killed in an automobile accident. He kept seeing a head-on collision, a phone call that went unanswered because he wasn't home from work yet, and police showing up at the door, asking him to identify my body. To avoid upsetting me, he didn't share this information.

Every day the premonition came back, always at different times. He kept calling me at work to see how I was doing, but I had no idea why. I just thought he was being sweet.

Finally, he decided that every time he got the premonition, he would tweak it by envisioning a different outcome. First he visualized that I didn't die; I lay in a hospital bed in a coma. Then he visualized I was in the hospital but would recover, and next that I was hurt, but not badly enough to be sent to the hospital. Finally, he envisioned that my car hit another, but that I walked away from the accident. This went on for several weeks.

Then one morning he woke up and thought, "It's going to happen today." Again he kept this to himself.

I remember it was one of those rare days that I could actually leave work at five o'clock. As a result, I encountered more traffic than usual. I was driving home completely unaware of what a miserable few weeks Stephen had endured. There were two lines of cars queuing up to a traffic light in an industrial area near where we live. I was in the left lane, which was moving along at a brisk pace. Shielded from view by a line of stopped cars in the right lane was a corporate driveway. A black car suddenly pulled out in front of me from that driveway. A stopped car to my right had blocked our view of each other. In the split second before the collision, I knew I would not have the time to avoid hitting the other car. The rest of the accident transpired in an eerie slow motion. I slammed on the brakes, swerving my car to the left to avoid hitting the other driver's car door, striking her front wheel instead.

My last thought before the impact was, "This is going to hurt." My small Saturn smashed into the side of the other car. I heard a bang and the halted momentum punched my entire body.

Airbags bloomed, blocking my view as metal crunched metal, and I flew forward toward the cushioned steering wheel then back against my seat. It was over in seconds. I sat there stunned. The airbag still acted as a blindfold, and it took a while to deflate. I had no idea how serious the accident had been or how badly anyone had been hurt.

Eventually, I staggered out of the car and noticed the other driver, a young girl, was still sitting in her car. She got out, too, and we both walked, a bit dazed, to the side of the road. She took out her cell phone and began making calls. I sat on some grass, in shock, staring at my feet. I didn't have a cell phone at the time, so the girl lent me hers to call Stephen. She told me this was her second accident at that same spot in three months; someone else had also broadsided her as she pulled out into traffic. ("Slow learner," I thought.)

Stephen answered my call, and I expected him to be surprised and upset. Instead, he said, "Oh, thank God. It's over. Are you okay?" I wanted more sympathy, but all he shared was his sense of relief. I hung up and waited for him to drive out and give me a ride home.

In the meantime, I received no sympathy from onlookers at the crash scene. The accident-prone young lady wore a short, tight-fitting black dress. Despite her poor driving record, male coworkers and the responding police officer rushed over to offer her fawning support. Middle-aged women, apparently, did not elicit the same degree of oozing concern. Fortunately, the insurance companies did not see it that way, finding her 100 percent at fault. My car was totaled. (Naturally, since it was my first new car in eleven years.)

It took me about six months to recover from the back and neck pain that announced itself the following day, but I was otherwise unhurt. The remains of my new car were towed to a junkyard and eventually replaced with a used one of the same color and model. And Stephen, after weeks of unrelenting worry finally got a good night's sleep.

Changing Fate
Thousands of precognitive experiences—where someone foresees a future event—were analyzed by Dr. Louisa Rhine at the Duke University Parapsychology Laboratory. She found that most precognitive experiences occurred in dreams, and 60 percent of those were vividly realistic. Even more interesting, she discovered in reviewing cases of people who tried to change the outcome they had foreseen, that only three people were successful. That may seem like very few, but Rhine makes the philosophical point that if a foreseen event can be averted even once, that means that the future is not immutable.

Normandy

Visions represent a subtle form of spiritual nagging if they are repetitive, but when the time is right, their meaning can unfold.

In 2011 Stephen began having a recurring vision of a hand reaching out of a sand dune and a voice crying, "Help me!" He didn't connect the vision with anything at that time because he was busy at work and his job preoccupied his thoughts.

A few months later we left for a vacation aboard the *Queen Mary 2* that included a visit to Normandy. During the transatlantic crossing from New York to Southampton, England, the disturbing vision began to increase in frequency and intensity. Stephen finally began to contemplate what it might mean.

Many people of my generation have parents who fought in World War II in Europe, Africa, and the Pacific. Those who returned carried with them stories of their trials on the battlefield. Those who didn't were often laid to rest in cemeteries halfway around the world from home. During our trip we visited one such cemetery near Omaha Beach in France.

Our journey brought us to several locations in which D-Day, then known as the Battle of Normandy, took place, including Pointe du Hoc, Omaha Beach, Utah Beach, and Sainte Mère Église.

On June 6, 1944, Allied Forces—Canadian, British, and American troops—landed on the beaches of Normandy. Their task was to push the German troops out of France and back into Germany. The D-Day invasion involved 5,000 ships carrying 150,000 men and 30,000 war vehicles across the English Channel, as well as 800 planes dropping six parachute regiments, totaling more than 13,000 paratroopers. More than 60 percent of the men who landed on the beaches that day died.

During our excursion to Pointe du Hoc, we viewed a point of land where American Rangers landed one hour before the invasion to scale one hundred-foot cliffs with grappling hooks. They did this while under machine-gun fire from German soldiers shooting from the safety of concrete bunkers.

The French have not touched Pointe du Hoc since 1944. It is considered hallowed ground. Today visitors can still see the concrete bunkers as well as the craters left by Allied bombers and ships that shelled the coastline during that battle.

While we were touring the American D-Day sites, Stephen began to understand the context of the message he had been receiving. As we walked around the memorial near Utah Beach, I spotted a sign that pointed the way to a path leading out to the ocean. I could hear the gentle waves rhythmically washing on the beach as we approached the sand. It was a pleasantly breezy day and the sea air was refreshing.

Utah Beach, a D-Day site in Normandy, France.

49

Stephen's experience was distinctly different from mine.

As we made our way down the path to the beach, he could hear a voice scream out again, "Help me!" He walked down to the surf, and when he turned to look back at the beach, he saw the hand from his vision sticking out of the same sand dune.

"The voice was so loud, it was almost booming," he said. He didn't know if the remains of any soldiers were still in the sand, but he was fairly certain that the French authorities would not appreciate his digging up sacred grounds to find out. So he sent out a psychic message to any departed soldiers lingering nearby to follow him and he would cross them over to the white light. This offer of help was to any souls still on the beach or in the waters at any of the sites we had visited that day.

We finished our tour and returned to the *Queen Mary 2*. After a full day of hiking in the crisp autumn air, sleep came easily to both of us. Around one in the morning, Stephen opened his eyes because he felt a presence in our stateroom.

"I was thinking there must be someone here; maybe that soldier came back with me," he said.

He was not unaccustomed to the feeling of spirits following him. When his sleepy eyes adjusted, he had to blink a couple of times because he wasn't sure whether what he was seeing was real. Not only was the soldier who had cried out to him standing in front of him, but about a dozen or so more were there, all in military uniforms of differing branches and nations. They looked down and saluted Stephen. He saluted back. The soldiers then turned around, walked through the wall, and disappeared. There were several rows of them, so he didn't know exactly how many passed through.

For more than sixty years, those departed soldiers had been waiting to go home. They just needed help crossing over. Stephen felt a profound sense of gratitude at being able to assist them.

Once again, this all transpired while I slept, undisturbed and oblivious, by his side.

Invisible Hitchhiker

When traveling, hitchhikers can come in the strangest forms, from viruses to vermin to people. Another type of freeloader can also attach itself onto an unsuspecting traveler, and this story is about one such vagabond—a spirit hitchhiker.

During a visit to Puerto Rico in 2008, Stephen picked up an uninvited companion. It was toward the end of a family vacation, and he was feeling a bit depressed about some personal matters. As we walked down the brightly colored streets of Old San Juan, the sky suddenly opened up and buckets of rain poured down.

Our family dashed into a nearby church for cover. Once inside, we decided to make the best of things. So we dropped some money in a donation box and set off to explore the historic building. Perhaps because of his emotional state, Stephen was vulnerable to attracting an unwanted spirit groupie. After our brief tour of the church, we lit candles for Stephen's mom and grandmother and my dad and grandmother, all departed. Eventually the rain abated, we left the church, and we cut short our humid sightseeing with a retreat to our air-conditioned ship.

That evening, our final night on the ship, Stephen began to smell stale cigarette smoke. Initially he assumed it was from people puffing away nearby. He was sitting in the library, a nonsmoking area, and the stale tobacco seemed annoyingly strong to him. Because smoke has a tendency to cling to clothes and upholstery, he assumed the odor had drifted in from the hallway.

But even after we returned home to New Jersey the next day, Stephen continued to smell the odor of cigarettes, despite the fact that no one in our family smoked. He noticed that an essence of old tobacco followed him everywhere he went—even to work—and began to increase in intensity. As the week progressed, the odor began to take on an acrid

The interior of the church
we toured in Puerto Rico.

quality, burning Stephen's eyes. Other people near him could now smell it.

Around the clock, wherever he was, smoke filled Stephen's nostrils. It no longer smelled stale but as though someone had just lit up. The odor was becoming a distraction both to him and his coworkers.

Stephen is a floor manager at an independent bookstore. Many of his coworkers are psychic—a strange coincidence. One of them, Regina, is particularly attuned to Stephen's psychic energy. Stephen asked Regina if she could see anyone around him, because he knew something wasn't right. Regina replied that she sensed he had picked up a spirit hitchhiker while in Puerto Rico. She suggested that if he closed his eyes and concentrated, he would be able to see the unwelcome guest.

After a few moments of concentration, Stephen saw a tall, emaciated, brown-skinned man with gray hair and a scraggly gray beard. He was smoking a cigarette. Regina, sensing his presence, asked his name, and he told her it was Zachary. He said he attached himself to Stephen so that he could see New York. Unfortunately, that was not going to happen since Stephen lived in New Jersey. It soon became clear, however, that Zachary had in mind another hidden purpose.

Stephen asked him what he wanted. Zachary told Stephen to speak to his father and forgive him. Regina advised Stephen to call his father, talk with him, and forgive him for whatever he might have done in the past.

The smoke died down after that, but there was an occasional whiff of it here and there, so Stephen knew the spirit was still hanging around.

A week later, on a Sunday, Stephen called his father to wish him an early happy

Why do you think that some people have such strong negative reactions to those who say they believe in and/ or have experienced psychic phenomena?

"It's due to conditioning, religious doctrine, or fear— maybe all three. We're all faced with mortality, and there's a fear about that. Receptiveness to the idea that there's something else out there, other than religious doctrine or nothing after life, is due to how we're raised. That's why children can see ghosts until they're told they aren't real."

—Stephen

birthday and told him about Zachary. Stephen apologized for anything he may have done in the past and said he forgave his father for the same. His father laughed. They had an hour phone conversation—the first such lengthy call he had ever had with his father. Stephen and his father had never been very close, and there had occasionally been some animosity between them. They both enjoyed their talk so much that they agreed when his father returned from a trip to Connecticut the following week they would get together for dinner. It was a breakthrough for both of them, and Stephen felt incredibly good about it. He wished his father a happy seventy-seventh birthday and hung up.

"After that call I felt light. We'd bridged a chasm that had long been between us," he said.

The following Saturday, quite unexpectedly, Stephen's father had a heart attack and passed away. Stephen was stunned.

"For some reason Zachary was there to guide this healing between us, and after that, I never sensed him again," he said. Stephen felt a sense of loss—he and his dad would never have that dinner. But at least they had found some closure before he left, and that's a great deal more than many estranged fathers and sons ever achieve.

CHAPTER 5

FLICKERS FROM THE OTHER SIDE

The intuitive mind is a sacred gift, and the rational mind is a faithful servant. We have created a society that honors the servant and has forgotten the gift.
—Albert Einstein, German-born theoretical physicist (1879–1955)

Young Connie is flanked by her father, Angelo, and mother, Dolores.

Connie

Losing the Hub

Some people are the hub of their families, holding everyone together. Stephen's mother, Connie, was one such person. She was a devout Catholic who also believed in reincarnation and had the wonderful quality of rarely judging other people. When she died just before Christmas in 2002, after a grueling five-month battle with leukemia, everyone in the family was devastated.

At her wake we all milled around in the funeral home, feeling lost. We simply couldn't believe she was gone.

Our sister-in-law, Francine, looked up at the ceiling and said, "Ma, give us a sign." Immediately the lights in the funeral home went out for about fifteen seconds.

If that wasn't enough, later that day at the traditional repast, Stephen's brother, Tom, asked once again if Mom could give us a sign. The lights of the restaurant flickered on cue, and we all knew, with a sense of longing, that she was intangibly with us.

Well-Adjusted Dead

Psychic mediums such as George Anderson and Echo Bodine often advise the grieving to wait at least six months to a year after their loved one passes to try to contact them. Just as those left behind must adjust to the departed's absence, the newly dead need time to get used to their existence on the other side. What I've observed from interviewing people for this book is that some spirits adjust rather quickly, reaching out almost immediately to their loved ones, and others take time. Perhaps more evolved or determined souls need less of an adjustment period.

Postcards from Beyond

After Connie passed away, Stephen desperately wanted to hear from her and asked her for a message. He got several.

The first was a few days after she was buried. He dreamt that he was in the funeral home. She lay in her casket, looked up at him, and asked, "Why am I here?"

"You're dead," he responded. That was the extent of the message. It was not the most comforting of dreams, but it was meaningful to Stephen.

About six months later Stephen decided to raid the refrigerator for a midnight snack. As he entered the kitchen, he saw his mother standing there. She wore a black dress with a string of pearls that she usually reserved for special occasions. The first thing he noticed about her was that she looked well, with no visible signs of the disease that had ravaged her.

"She just stood there and smiled at me," he said. "She was showing me that she was fine and back to being who she was. I waved. She hung out for about ten minutes while I got myself a snack, and then she finally faded away."

About a year after his mother's death, Stephen was in bed one night and found himself transported far away, out of body, to a French bistro.

"There was a café outside," Stephen said. "The sun was shining. It was warm. I was in an old-fashioned European village. People were milling about. I was sitting at a small table, and my mother came over and joined me.

"We chatted," he said. "I don't remember what we talked about. She looked younger. She was wearing that black dress again, with those beautiful pearls. It felt good to see that she was okay and looked well. She told me that she was happy and that everything was fine—not to worry. We just sat there and had tea and lunch. When it was time to go, she got up and walked into the crowd. The next thing you know I woke up. If that was a dream, it was the most vivid dream I've ever had."

Messages from Connie

Messages from beyond can be funny, profound, or startling. Sometimes they can be all three.

Connie had a difficult life. Her father died when she was a young adult, so she found herself helping to raise some of her siblings and working to help support the household.

She often told people that she didn't remember having a childhood. Married life presented even more responsibilities and trials. So it was no surprise to those who knew her when she would say, "If I had to do it all over again, I wouldn't!" It was a wise-cracking mantra she often recited with a smirk at family gatherings.

When Connie was sixty-nine, she developed a persistent fever that was diagnosed as acute leukemia; she died shortly after her seventieth birthday. It was a terrible shock to everyone, particularly considering that Connie's mother was still alive and would live to be a few months shy of one hundred, and her grandmother had lived to be ninety-seven.

When Stephen's mother died, he was inconsolable. To help ease his grief, I arranged a session with a psychic medium on Long Island. This medium is well known for relaying messages from the dead to mourning relatives and friends. He also dedicates himself to helping parents cope with grief when they lose a child.

We sat in a small hotel meeting room in New York with several other people hoping to hear from departed loved ones. We waited, patiently, for Stephen's mother to come through. Finally, she did. She told Stephen to send love to her sister Anna and that she was hanging out with her friend Rose, who had died a year before her.

As the session closed, the medium said, "Oh wait, she has one more message for you." His brows knitted uncomprehendingly, but he relayed the message anyway. "I don't know if this means anything to you, but she says that if she had to do it all over again... she would."

Tom

Stephen's youngest brother Tom also inherited the psychic gene. A tall, dark-haired man who savors life and loves a party, he was a bit wild in his youth but eventually settled down with his soul mate, Francine.

Party Crasher

Italians love family, so family gatherings are important. Birthdays, weddings, funerals, and other significant events are marked by everyone getting together to celebrate or mourn. That attendance is by no means confined to the living.

Francine planned a surprise party for Tom's fortieth birthday. The guests parked down the street when they arrived so Tom wouldn't suspect anything. We all huddled in the living room, ready to spring up and yell "Surprise!" on cue.

How old were you when you had your first psychic experience?

"I was probably twenty-six. I was talking to a man as I walked down the street. Then he said, 'I have to go, Tom,' and just disappeared."

—Tom

When Tom finally walked through the door, he got more of a surprise than was planned.

"The first person I saw when I walked into the room was my godfather, Dennis," Tom said. A tall, lanky man, he often stood out in a crowd. There was nothing unusual about that.

"But standing right next to Dennis in the corner of the dining room was my mother wearing a beige sweater," he said. "She had a big smile." He got only a brief glimpse of her before she disappeared, but it was nice to know that she had not missed his milestone birthday party.

Knock, Knock

Both Tom and Francine have noticed that whenever Connie visits from the other side, a scent of flowers fills the room, faintly reminiscent of lilacs.

One night back in 2003, Tom locked the front door of the house then went into the family room to relax.

"It was Halloween, about a year after Mom passed away," he said. As he lay on the couch watching television, he fell asleep. Francine and their son Tommy Jr. went upstairs to bed.

"I woke up a little after midnight and smelled a strong odor of flowers in the room," he said. Tom got up, turned off the television, and noticed the front door was open. He moved slowly toward it, opened it the rest of the way, and looked outside. No one was there.

"I closed it and went to bed," he said. "I don't know if Mom came to visit and departed, but if she did, she left the door wide open!" He said he looks forward to future visits, but hopes when they occur, she will remember to lock up before she leaves. Perhaps this time she simply wanted to make sure he knew she'd been there.

Tom, in a quiet moment,
during a family gathering.

> ### Scent of a Loved One
> Sensing the dead through smell is called clairalience (also, clairescence). The dead, says psychic medium Echo Bodine, think of a scent that their loved ones would associate with them and then project it. It's just another way they communicate. Paranormal researchers Bill and Judy Guggenheim found in the people they interviewed that the most common scents associated with a departed loved one were fragrances, such as perfume, cologne, or aftershave; flowers; food or beverages; or tobacco.

All's Well

Sometimes parents like to let their children know everything is all right—even after death. Tom had a dream that affirmed that for him. His father died seven years after his mother. A year after his father passed, he received an unscheduled visit from him in his sleep.

"Our doorbell rang," he said. "I answered the door, and it was my father with his girlfriend. We weren't expecting anyone, so I was surprised. After Mom died, Dad rarely came by to visit us." But his father stood there, wearing a flannel shirt and pants, partially covered by a beige raincoat.

"We were in the neighborhood and decided to stop by," his father said as he walked over the threshold. His girlfriend followed, but as she entered the house, she suddenly turned into Tom's mother. His mother was wearing a skirt and sweater that peeked through her open, light blue raincoat.

"I said to her, 'What are you doing here?'" Tom said. His mom smiled and replied rather matter-of-factly that she wanted to visit.

"They both looked very joyful to be stopping by together," he said. Tom felt that this was his parents' way of letting him know that they had reunited on the other side and all was well.

Francine

Francine is the perfect complement to Tom. Passionate about life, she enjoys socializing and is a gracious hostess. Clearly, she married into the right clan because she is very psychic.

Backseat Driving

Family members never stop caring about each other, even after death. They may whisper a word of comfort or a suggestion in the ears of their living kin or even manifest a distraction to alter a relative's behavior for the better. Here is a story about one such occurrence.

Connie apparently takes an active interest in our family from her vantage point on the other side. Francine remembered one day when she received some roadside assistance from her departed mother-in-law.

Francine offers the peace-out sign while preparing daiquiris.

"I'm driving home from work, and I stop at a light," Francine said. Her car was in the right side of two lanes of traffic waiting for the light to turn green. A green minivan was pulled up beside her in the left lane, also waiting to cross the intersection.

"Typically, when the light turns green, I hit the gas and go. I don't look around." But on this day, something made her hesitate when the light turned. She looked down at her hand on the steering wheel and saw that her wedding ring had turned into her late mother-in-law's engagement ring. At the same time, she sensed someone sitting in the seat behind her.

"I glanced up into the rearview mirror, and I saw Connie sitting in the middle of the back seat in a blue housedress with flowers on it. She had a little smile on her face." Suddenly, the sounds of tires screeching and metal crunching drew her attention back to the intersection. The green minivan had zoomed ahead and was hit broadside by a large SUV that had run the light.

"Had I hit the gas as I usually do, the SUV would have run into my passenger side and decapitated me," Francine said. "I pulled over to call the police. I almost didn't know if I could drive home, I was so shaken."

After witnessing the accident, her wedding ring changed back to her own, and Connie was gone. But to this day Francine credits her late mother-in-law with saving her life.

Early Warning System

Paranormal researchers Bill and Judy Guggenheim interviewed a number of people whose lives had been saved by a communication with a dead relative. Most mediums will tell you that our departed relatives have an ongoing interest in the living they've left behind and may try to warn them if something bad is about to happen. The three most common messages received by the people the Guggenheims interviewed were a sign that helped prevent a car accident, a warning about a serious medical condition requiring immediate attention, and an early alert about a fire.

Dragonflies

Sometimes the most profound messages we receive from the other side are as ephemeral as their sources. Francine had an experience one hot summer day that bore that out.

"I was going to see a customer up in Jersey City," Francine said. "Usually I don't stop by the cemetery to visit Connie's grave unless Tom is with me, but I had an overwhelming feeling to visit there." It was a sunny day in late July. When she got to the grave, she saw something unusual.

"There were thousands of dragonflies all over the place around her tombstone and grave," she said. "They were translucent blues and greens, reflecting in the sun. You could see their shadows on the gravestone. I took a picture with my phone, but none of the dragonflies showed up. I also smelled Connie's floral scent."

How old were you when you had your first psychic experience?

"I was nineteen. I was living at my grandfather's house after he had passed away. The lights would dim a little bit, and you could sense that he was there."

—Francine

In many cultures around the world, the dragonfly symbolizes change as it pertains to self-realization. In particular, it represents the kind of change that comes with mental and emotional maturity and an understanding of the deeper meaning of life. Was Connie showing Francine a symbol of her spiritual progress on the other side? Or was she expressing her affection for her daughter-in-law?

"I have never seen dragonflies at the gravesite before or since. I was only there about fifteen minutes, but I felt very calm when I left. It was as if she were with me."

Tommy Jr.

Our nephew, Tommy Jr., inherited his parents' spirited sense of fun as well as their unique perspective on life. From the time he was a toddler, he showed himself to be one of the most psychically gifted members of our family. The following stories, as told by his mother, illustrate why.

Relatives Past

Veterans' Day in November is a time for showing respect to those who fought to keep our country safe. In most cemeteries local organizations place flags on the graves of departed soldiers.

November also happens to be the month of Connie's birthday, so family members often visit her grave then to remember her. One chilly November day when Tom, Francine, and Tommy Jr. were visiting Connie's grave, a very young Tommy Jr. started taking flags from the surrounding graves and began placing them on the grave of one man nearby.

"Tommy Jr. was two years old," Tom said. "It shocked us. We told him, 'You can't do that. They're veterans.' He said he was sorry."

"We had no idea why he was doing that," Francine said. Neither one of them was familiar with the name on the tombstone. Out of curiosity they took down the information. Later they found out from Aunt Anna that the grave was the final resting place of an ancestor who had been a World War II veteran. So it turned out that in his own way, Tommy Jr. had been observing the holiday by honoring a deceased family member.

Last Laugh

At some point in childhood, children are introduced to the concept of death and funerals. A few years after his Nana Connie died, Tommy Jr.'s Great-Grandma Dolores passed away. While he had not attended his Nana Connie's wake, this time his parents decided he was old enough to visit the funeral home.

The week before, Tommy Jr. had visited Dolores in the nursing home and heard her say she wanted to die. Francine observed her son turning and pointing to the empty doorway of the room, in response, and saying, "Great-Grandma wants to be with Nana because Nana is here."

A week later Great-Grandma Dolores was gone.

At the wake Tommy Jr. looked around the room with a sense of wonder and told Francine, "I have a lot of dead family members."

The next day the family traveled to Jersey City to attend the funeral service. The cemetery is quite large and contains many internal roads, as well as being divided in the middle by a public throughway. When they arrived, Tom pulled into one of the internal roads in search of the funeral when Tommy Jr. informed him that he was going in the wrong direction.

"Nana says we're going the wrong way," Tommy Jr. said. "Nana is laughing because we're on the wrong side of the cemetery." It turns out that they were.

The Crystal Bell

Collecting seems to run in Stephen's family. His mother collected spoons and bells. After her death, the bell collection was packed in a box, which came to rest in Tom and Francine's garage.

During Christmas season in 2011, when Tommy Jr. was ten, his grandparents came by for another visit, and one of them apparently had a request for their grandson.

"Tommy was lying on the couch with a glazed look on his face," Francine said. She was standing nearby and noticed their dog's tail was wagging. The animal began barking at something near the fireplace.

"Nana doesn't like dogs," Tommy Jr. commented. Then speaking to the empty space near the fireplace, he added, "I *am* a good boy. Did you see my swim meet?"

"Tommy, who are you talking to?" Francine asked.

"Pop-Pop," he replied.

Tommy Jr. walked toward the hallway and Francine followed him.

"Tommy looked me square in the face and said, 'I want the bell.'" Francine knew he was referring to his Nana's bell collection, but she had no idea which one he wanted or in which box it was packed in the garage.

"I want the bell, and Pop-Pop says the pictures are old and you have to replace them," he said, pointing at his old baby pictures on the wall. "You're so silly," he said, continuing to talk to someone invisible. "He says I'm trouble, but they're so proud of me with my swimming."

"Several times Tommy has told us that Pop-Pop came to watch his swim meet," Francine said.

When Tom came downstairs to join them, Tommy Jr. looked at his father and repeated, "Get me the bell." Without much thought, Tom went into the garage, opened a box, reached in, and retrieved a glass bell from his mother's collection. It was made out of crystal, with red diamond shapes on its handle. Tom has described it as resembling an upside-down wine glass.

"That's it!" Tommy Jr. exclaimed. "Nana said this is her bell!" He told his parents that he had seen his Nana, and that she was wearing a gray housecoat and her brown glasses. That night Tommy Jr. slept peacefully, his Nana's crystal bell clutched in his hands.

CHAPTER 6

Mysterious Encounters of Psychic Bystanders

Don't believe what your eyes are telling you. All they show is limitation. Look with your understanding, find out what you already know, and you'll see the way to fly.

—Richard Bach, American writer (1936–)

Alfred

My father, Alfred, belonged to what has sometimes been called the Greatest Generation. A World War II veteran, he returned home after the war, married, had two children, and spent a great deal of time involved in local politics and social justice issues. He really cared about those less fortunate and was a great role model and dad.

Alfred, who served as a corporal, Eleventh Airborne Division, Company 188.

Aerial View

Great psychic abilities don't run in my family. But it's said that most people have the ability to be psychic; some just have more of a natural aptitude than others.

My father, who did not believe in anything psychic, had one experience that he shared only with my mother, because he wasn't comfortable with it.

Toward the end of his life, he endured six heart bypasses. After years of smoking, his cardiovascular system was not in good condition.

During one operation something happened that startled him. He rose up out of his body during the surgery and watched the operation from above. He felt sure that it was not his imagination, because he saw things that he felt were beyond his personal experience. I didn't find out about this until years after he'd passed, when my mother finally shared it with me.

Mystical Statistics
In the early 1970s Andrew M. Greeley, director of the Center for the Study of American Pluralism, National Opinion Research Center, was commissioned by the Henry Luce Foundation to conduct a national study on basic belief systems. Several questions in this study were directed specifically at psychic experiences. Researchers assumed the response would be low. To their surprise almost a fifth of the 1,500 respondents reported frequent paranormal experiences. The study concluded that "paranormal is normal." Here are some of their findings:

- Nearly 60 percent had experienced déjà vu (familiarity with a place where they had never been)
- Nearly 60 percent had experienced extrasensory perception (in touch with someone far away)
- Nearly one in four had experienced clairvoyance (seeing events happen at a great distance as they were happening)
- More than one in four felt they had been in contact with a loved one who had died
- Overall, psychics were less likely to be racist and had greater confidence in their spiritual beliefs than those with no psychic experiences

Louisa

I have portrayed myself as a psychic bystander, and for the most part, that is precisely how I feel. Everyone around me, both family and friends, seems to have spectacular premonitions, astounding visits from the departed, and/or incredible out-of-body excursions. I, on the other hand, tend to be fairly earthbound and rarely experience anything otherworldly.

I've had only a few episodes in life that can be classified as psychic, and they usually occurred when I was in a semiwaking state. Still, they happened, and my thoughts are that if I can experience these things, anyone can. So here are my stories.

The Guardian

Many years ago I lived in an apartment in Boonton, New Jersey. One night, in a half-awake state, I looked up and thought I saw a man covered in a brown sheet, staring at me from across the room. That struck me as extremely odd, but for some reason I felt no fear. When I called out to him, the figure disappeared. Upon reflection I realized that the figure that had visited me was a monk. His face had been obscured by the drooping hood that he wore. I didn't get any sense that he was there to harm me; he was just watching over me.

I soon forgot the experience, until another night several years later after I had moved from the Boonton apartment into my first house with my husband. I awoke in the middle of the night to see the same hooded figure across from my bed, staring at me. As I became conscious enough to recognize the monk, he disappeared.

Perhaps he was a guardian. I never saw the figure again.

Ungrateful Dead

I'm not a fan of scary movies. You'll never get me into a cinema to see one, because I'm essentially a coward—and quite comfortable with it. So frightening experiences are especially difficult for me. One such event imposed itself on me many years ago when I lived in an apartment in Boonton on Cedar Street. The building sat directly across from St. Cyril and Methodius Cemetery. I never gave it much thought until one night when an unwelcome visitor came calling.

My bedroom faced the cemetery. At the foot of the bed was a television, and behind that was a window that looked out onto the graves across the way.

One night I roused sometime after midnight in a semiconscious state. That was unusual for me, because I'm a sound sleeper. My eyes were closed, but I could see the room as clearly as if they were open.

The television, which was turned off, suddenly lit up with white, crackling static, partially illuminating the room in an eerie white glow. I sensed that someone was at the window, which was odd because the room was on the second floor. He was trying to enter but couldn't. Some sort of barrier was holding him back. He seemed angry because he was dead and I was living. I felt his anger pierce through the glass and became frightened. My body, however, couldn't move. I was frozen in place. I lay there for several very long minutes.

Eventually, the static on the television died down and the angry apparition faded away. He never came back, which was fine with me.

St. Cyril and Methodius Cemetery located in Boonton, New Jersey.

Paradise Lost

I suppose that a meditative state can also count as being half-awake. Once, when I was in my twenties, I sat cross-legged on my bed on the second floor of my parent's home in Boonton. I went into a very deep meditation and went out of body and into a strange world.

I was flying, and there were others at my side. I couldn't see them, but I could sense them. It was daytime. The skies were purple and there were three suns above. I experienced a sense of freedom that was unparalleled in the physical world. And there was total peace. Then, this tiny thought crept into my mind: wasn't I sitting on my bed in my room at home?

Immediately, I snapped back into my body. I was fully awake, so I know it wasn't a dream. My astral adventure felt as real as the physical world to which I returned. I have never experienced anything like it since.

Reconnecting

There are dreams, and then there are vivid dreams. Once you've encountered the latter, you know that it has very little to do with a normal sleep experience.

My father's death back in 1995 left a real void in my life. I wondered how he was doing and if he even existed anymore. One night I fell asleep and had a lucid dream. I was walking in a beautiful, natural landscape. The colors were so vivid that they surpassed the more muted colors we see in the physical world. My father was there, and we walked together and had a long conversation. I don't remember what we said, but I do recall knowing that Dad was fine. The countryside we strolled through imparted a sense of complete happiness—no worries, no cares, just total bliss. When the dream ended, I felt that I had actually spent some time with Dad. That feeling of absolute peace lasted for a few days afterward.

Lucid Dreams

More than 2,000 people were interviewed by paranormal researchers Bill and Judy Guggenheim about communications they had had with their departed loved ones. The Guggenheims found that there were distinct differences between regular dreams and lucid, or vivid, dreams. Regular dreams tended to be incoherent and incomplete in many ways. Lucid dreams, on the other hand, usually involved visits with departed relatives and friends and were more logical, detailed, and memorable.

The Signing

When loved ones die, even if you feel certain they have survived death and are doing well on the other side, it is still difficult not to miss them. The tangible part of the relationship—two-way conversations, a hug, a shared activity—are no longer possible. That is the essence of grief.

My father has been gone for more than seventeen years. We were very close. So when I stood in line at a book signing for Concetta

Bertoldi, a famous psychic medium from Boonton Township, New Jersey, I decided to ask if she could help me make contact with him.

I got to the front of the line and boldly inquired, "Hi, I hope this isn't too nervy to ask, but could you give me a minireading while you're signing my book?"

"Sure." She smiled. We had never met before, so her gesture was quite generous.

She cocked her head to one side then said, "Your father has passed."

"Yes," I said.

"His name was Al?"

"Yes."

"He says you have his military picture on your cell phone and on your desk at work."

"Yes, I do."

"He thanks you for that. He also says you turned out to be just like him, and he's proud of you." That's true; both he and I had shared a passion for social justice. I guess you could say I inherited my values from him.

It was a short reading, but a very reassuring one. I knew that he was out there and was watching over me.

Chelsea

Our younger daughter Chelsea is a petite blonde with mischievous blue eyes. Something of a bookworm, she's an unusually profound thinker, and I learn a lot from our conversations. She hasn't had many psychic experiences, but she does recall one from her college days that has stuck with her.

How old were you when you had your first psychic experience?

"I was nineteen years old. A ghost visited my apartment. I definitely told my roommate when she got home. I kind of freaked out."

—Chelsea

Ghost in the Shower

Seeing, it is said, is believing. But what if the sight one sees abruptly disappears?

While attending Montclair State University in 2005, Chelsea rented an apartment in nearby Clifton with a friend. While living there, she and her roommate Kelly always felt as though someone was watching them, although they couldn't explain why. Gradually they both became aware that when in the apartment, they experienced a subtle but distinctly heightened sense of anxiety.

One night Kelly blacked out in the shower and Chelsea ran in to help her. It was an unusual occurrence for Kelly. She was young and in perfectly good health. She had no idea what had brought it on.

A few weeks later, however, Chelsea received an unwelcome glimpse of what might have been behind her roommate's fainting episode. Chelsea was alone in the apartment and decided to take a shower to unwind from a long day. As the warm water relaxed her muscles, she began to feel a little light-headed. She closed her eyes and thought she saw the shadowy outline of a person standing in the stall with her. In a sudden motion, it reached out and grabbed her upper arms. Reflexively, Chelsea glanced down and saw bruises on her arms. Startled by this, adrenaline snapped her back to an alert state. She quickly exited the stall to dry herself and noticed that the marks on both of her arms were gone.

Several friends who visited the apartment in the year Chelsea and her roommate lived there commented that they also felt bad vibes on the premises. Neither girl was one to miss a cue; when the lease came up for renewal, they moved out.

Part II

Psychic Friends and Strangers

Psychic ability is far more common than people think. The second half of this book follows individuals from all walks of life, from business leaders and teachers to blue-collar workers, all of whom have psychic abilities. Chapter 7 highlights the stories of people I know. Friends of friends and psychic professionals are in the chapters that follow. Many of the people I interviewed had never before talked openly about their paranormal experiences with anyone. Several told me after we spoke that for the first time in their lives they felt validated and comfortable with their gift.

CHAPTER 7

FRIENDS WITH PSYCHIC BENEFITS

We should not pretend to understand the world only by the intellect. The judgment of the intellect is only part of the truth.

— Carl Jung, Swiss psychologist/psychiatrist (1875–1961)

Carol, Medical Auditor

Carol is one of my oldest friends. Her mother and my mother had the same doctor when they were pregnant. Both our mothers went into labor on Valentine's Day, and they kept the doctor very busy through the following morning. Carol entered the world first, and I followed about two and a half hours later.

The Visit

When children say they've seen or heard something that seems impossible, they are often scolded for lying. But what if they're telling the truth?

"When I was about thirteen, my sister Martha and I shared a bedroom," Carol said. "One night when we went to bed, the shades on the two windows in our room suddenly started going up and down, up and down." This didn't make much sense when you consider that not even the wind could have been a culprit, with both windows firmly shut.

"We got up really fast. Then we heard bells ringing and called our mom." Carol's mom came upstairs and wanted to know what all the commotion was about. No sooner had they finished telling her than the telephone rang.

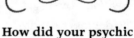

How did your psychic experience affect the way you thought about the world around you?

"I guess it made me feel that there was more to the world than you can see and touch. There's more than this life. That's how my mother explained it."

— Carol

77

"It was my aunt. She said my grandfather had passed away. My mother felt that what happened was that my grandfather had visited to say good-bye."

Joy, Registered Nurse

I first met Joy when we were in the fourth grade. A slim blonde with stylish short hair, she sat behind me in homeroom. We quickly became friends, and I grew up spending many after-school hours in her home with her family.

The Reprieve

For some people, premonitions can serve as a warning. For others, they can provide comfort during challenging times. This is a story about the latter.

In 2000, when Joy found out her father-in-law, Tony, had developed pancreatic cancer, she knew that the prognosis for the disease was very poor.

"It was an upsetting time," Joy said. Tony checked in to a hospital in New York for surgery, with his wife and Joy's husband, Jim, by his side. The doctors would need to determine the size of the tumor and whether there was any vascular involvement that might complicate the surgery.

"I was devastated," she said. "I couldn't focus on anything that day but him." She walked into the woods near her home to an overlook. It offered a panoramic view of the valley below that she found calming.

"I prayed for him and that the family would survive this," she said. She closed her eyes and meditated. As she did, she received a vision.

"I saw my father-in-law in the hospital. Two doctors were performing surgery, and one turned to the other and said, 'This looks good. The blood vessels are not involved. We can get the tumor out.' Then I saw a smile on my father-in-law's face. I went from feeling devastated to being totally at peace."

For the rest of the morning, Joy felt fine and waited for a phone call from the hospital.

"Jim called and what the surgeons told him was exactly what I had heard in my head." In the year that followed, Tony spent a great deal of time with his family, took a vacation, and generally enjoyed life.

"That's unusual for someone with pancreatic cancer," she said. "I had had a vision that there would be more quality time for us together, and thankfully, it came true."

Psychic Triggers

In the 1970s study discussed earlier in which 1,500 people were interviewed about their basic belief systems, the following activities were found to have triggered mystical experiences:

Listening to music	49%
Prayer	48%
Beauties of nature, such as sunsets	45%
Moments of quiet reflection	42%
Attending church services	41%
Listening to sermons	40%
Watching small children	34%
Reading the Bible	31%
Being alone in church	21%
Reading a poem or a novel	20%

Sign of the Eagle

A premonition offered comfort in the last story. Symbols can also offer reassurance during times of stress and grief.

Joy's father, Don, was a tall, muscular man who loved his family and loved life. It was difficult not to like him because he always showed such a genuine concern for everyone he met. Even as a child, I felt that he took my feelings and opinions seriously.

He was bald long before it was popular and had deep-set hazel eyes. In tribute to his appearance, his Citizens Band* radio handle was "Bald Eagle," and that nickname stuck. Up through his seventies, Don continued to lead a busy and physically active life.

"One Saturday morning, he and my mom were going to the bank,"

---

*Citizens Band (CB) radios were short-distance radios popular in the 1970s with truckers and commuters. Typically, drivers would warn each other about accidents, speed traps, and traffic jams. Users had a handle, or nickname, that they signed on with to identify themselves when talking with others. CBs have fallen out of favor in the general populace with the advent of cell phones.

Joy said. "On the way he had visual problems. When they got to the bank, he collapsed and they called an ambulance. By the time he arrived at the emergency room, he had lapsed into a coma."

Don had suffered a stroke. He was immediately placed on a ventilator with a feeding tube. His transition from wellness to a vegetative state happened so quickly that it left his family in shock.

"It was so unexpected," Joy said. "I was having a really hard time going through it and watching my mom go through it." Her mother sat next to his hospital bed for weeks, unwilling to leave his side.

"I was a basket case," she said. "My father-in-law was dying of pancreatic cancer at the same time. I would wake up in the morning and my pillow would be wet because I was crying in my sleep. Four or five days after the stroke, I woke up in the middle of the night." Not wanting to bother her husband, Joy went downstairs and tried to relax.

"I was sitting and praying," she said. Her biggest fear was that her father was fully conscious but unable to respond to anyone. The thought of such an active man trapped in an unresponsive body horrified her.

"I wanted to know that he was okay, that he wasn't suffering, even if he wasn't going to recover," she said. "I asked to receive some kind of sign." Because his nickname was Bald Eagle, she decided that whatever sign she received should be related to that image.

"After that, I felt better and went back to bed," she said. "The next morning I went out to the mailbox to pick up the newspaper. When I opened it up, there was a large picture of a bald eagle with its wings outstretched on the front page." She had been so preoccupied with her father's condition that she had forgotten that the day before had been an election day. On the top of each page of that edition, along with the election results, was a small eagle.

How old were you when you had your first psychic experience?

"I was forty-five. I told people about it—mostly my family and close friends. I felt comforted. I knew there was something more to this life than what we see here."
—Joy

"I thought, 'Maybe this really does mean something,'" she said. The image of an eagle was in the papers for weeks after that, because the 2000 presidential election was not immediately settled.

"It gave me a good feeling," she said. "I never told my mother about the sign, because I didn't want to upset her. After my dad passed, we met with the priest at my mom's church to discuss arrangements." Her mother needed to choose songs for the service. She told the priest she had already selected them. At the top of the list was a hymn called "On Eagles' Wings."

"I was shocked that Mom had picked that song," she said. "She told me it was my dad's favorite hymn at church.

"Even to this day, when I'm upset about something, I will see an eagle somewhere. Shortly after Dad died, I was over my mother's house helping her clean, and at one point she started crying. I went over, put my arms around her, and I'm thinking, 'What do I do to comfort this woman?' As I was hugging her, the television in the kitchen flashed on a commercial that caught my eye. There was an eagle gliding across the screen."

Jo, Price Development Manager

I first met Jo in seventh grade homeroom. I turned around and saw a young girl sitting behind me with her hair pulled back in a long, dark braid. Jo was born in the Calabria region of Italy and moved to the United States when she was eight months old. During her childhood, she heard many stories from the Old Country that had been passed down through her family. She shares two that stand out in her memory.

Graveyard Shift

Life and death take on a special significance in times of war, sometimes blurring the line between the two.

It was World War I. Jo's uncle Giuseppe, at the age of eighteen, had

Jo offers an intriguing art shot.

enlisted in the army and was fighting in Northern Italy against the Germans and Austro-Hungarians. Whenever they weren't in the battlefield, he and his fellow soldiers played cards and smoked, perhaps the only two forms of relaxation available while off duty. As the card players' shifts came up, they were called to the battlefield. Those who left were replaced by the men who were returning from combat, making the card game continuous.

As the story goes, Jo said, "During a late night card game, one of the players, Guglielmo, came back from battle and was very quiet, pale, and withdrawn. Everyone was smoking, except Guglielmo, which was unusual because he enjoyed his tobacco. They asked him if he was all right, and he said he was."

On the next shift, Guglielmo left and Jo's uncle Giuseppe went to sleep for the night.

"The next morning, the roster came in on who had been wounded, killed, or deserted during the previous day," Jo said. "Guglielmo was listed as killed, which meant that the night before, my uncle and his friends had played cards with a dead man."

How old were you when you had your first psychic experience?

"I was thirteen. I had taken a detour to avoid passing someone's house and was walking down a side street that my father used to walk with me when he took me to the park. My father had recently died, and I remember saying, 'I miss you, Daddy.' Just then, I smelled the aftershave he used to wear on Sundays, and it was a Sunday."

—Jo

What If They Gave a Thought and Nobody Came?

War has been with us since before recorded history. It seems embedded in our way of thinking. And perhaps that's the problem. Everything in the physical world begins with a thought, write Silvia Cranston and Carey Williams in their book *Reincarnation: A New Horizon in Science, Religion, and Society*. War is no exception. James Van Praagh agrees in his book *Ghosts Among Us*. He writes that thoughts are living entities as solid as a rock or a chair. Thoughts have an effect on our lives and on the lives of those around us. He adds that after we die, thoughts are part of the life review and we are held accountable for them. If what Cranston, Williams, and Van Praagh are saying is true, swaying the thoughts of a populace could change the world.

Disturbing the Dead

Animals have a special sensitivity to the unseen world around us, as illustrated in the following story.

During World War II, all the men in most of the smaller villages in Italy were gone, except a few who had special civilian duties. One night there was a minor earthquake near Jo's hometown of Marcellinara, Italy.

"An old man in the village delivered supplies on his mule every day," Jo said. "In the wee hours of the morning, he tried to get his mule through town, but the animal was leaning and scraping itself against the medieval village walls. The mule was afraid to walk in the middle of the road. The man started beating the mule and screaming at him because he was going to be late for a delivery. But above him, old lady Donna Rachella, who was known to be psychic, leaned out her window and shouted, 'Stop beating that poor animal. Can't you see? He can't walk. The street's too crowded with dead people.'"

In a town nearby, while no one had been killed, the earthquake had caused an upheaval in an old cemetery. That geologic event, Jo said, had apparently unsettled the dead and sent their spirits wandering through the streets.

Keith, Former DJ, Green Grocer

Keith was my college roommate's younger brother. I still remember him as an adorable eleven-year-old, whom I "adopted" as my little brother. He grew up to become a popular DJ in Washington, DC, and more recently took a steady job with a retail health food chain. He lives with his life partner, Jimmy.

Keeping in Touch

It's a cliché, but endings are often cleverly disguised beginnings. When Keith lost someone he loved, she introduced him to an entirely different way of viewing death. His life has never been the same since.

Keith was very close to his paternal grandmother, Granny Mac.

"She was a very happy woman who would laugh and sing old hymns off-key. She was just fun to be around," he said.

When Keith was sixteen, his grandmother became quite ill. She was dying on a respirator at the hospital, and he kept vigil by her side.

"I got to hold her hand in the hospital. It felt alternately cold and hot as she was leaving the planet." Finally, the temperature shifts stopped. She passed away soon after.

"It was unhappy for me, because I loved her very much and I knew my father would be upset," he said. But in retrospect, Keith now feels differently, perhaps because of what happened afterward. "Now I look back on it as one of the most beautiful moments in my life."

Keith drove home feeling devastated. He got up the next morning and had to go to work, even though the funeral was planned for the next day. Then, amid his misery, something comforting happened.

"My grandmother came to me and told me that the world was fine and she was okay,"

I remember Keith best as an eleven-year-old; he's grown.

Keith said. This was no half-conscious dream. He was awake when she visited. After that, he continued to see her periodically and still does to this day.

"I will see her on a street corner, or somewhere else she would never normally have been, in her favorite size 18 dress with her purse. I've seen my mom, too, although more often in dreams." When Granny Mac shows up, Keith said, she will wave or smile and then disappear.

"When I can smell the polyester dresses, the smell of her hairnet, or denture cream—when I pick up the scent—I know I will be seeing a glimpse of her and then she'll be gone." He said he's grateful that death did not sever their relationship.

Three's a Crowd

Was it a trick of the light or was there really something there? People often ask themselves that. In this story the answer seems to be the latter.

For the past three years, Keith and Jimmy have lived in Kingman Park, a neighborhood in Northeast Washington, DC, in the Stadium Armory district. Their building was constructed in 1933 during the Great Depression. It boasts beautiful rosewood floors, spacious rooms, and an enclosed porch.

Keith and Jimmy work different shifts, so they are rarely in the apartment at the same time.

How old were you when you had your first psychic experience?

"I've been alone in the house and Jimmy's been alone in the house, and we've both thought something was weird but didn't initially talk about it," Keith said. "We both saw something out of the corner of the eye. It was a three-dimensional, shadowy figure of a large man." Keith said he had no face or clothes—just a gray form.

"I was sixteen. My grandmother came by to let me know everything was all right after she passed away. I was really happy. I told my sister and dad about it. He chuckled about it at the time. Now he's much more in tune with it."

"If I look directly at it, it goes away," he said. "When we are lying in bed, every other room in the apartment is visible except the bathroom. We can see the form

—Keith

go from room to room, the way you would think people would, from the bedroom to the kitchen and then to the dining room. He never goes through doorways; he just walks through things."

They currently have an enclosed porch, but in earlier days it was screened.

"He must not like the renovation. He never goes there," Keith said.

They also have a third witness to their shadowy roommate: their Labradoodle dog, Titan. Whenever anyone talks to Titan, the dog looks that person straight in the eye and listens attentively until the speaker is finished. Usually, the recipients of this attention are Keith or Jimmy. Every so often, Titan will stare at the wall for an extended period of time with the same rapt attention he bestows on human conversation.

"Nothing is there," Keith said, "but Titan sits at attention, exactly as he does when we speak, cocking his head and listening intently. It must be a good spirit who likes dogs, because Titan clearly loves this person."

Zoë, LMT, Energy Healer, Spiritual Counselor

I first met Zoë when she was opening her healing center in Denville, New Jersey, and needed some materials written. We immediately formed a bond and have been friends ever since. That was more than twenty-five years ago.

Psychic in the Convent

Sometimes when someone knows too much, it can be annoying to others, especially if the know-it-all is a child.

Zoë was educated in a Catholic convent, where she lived until the age of fourteen. She was actually quite psychic as a child, which must have been a bit awkward in that environment.

"When I was six years old, I had the uncanny ability to tell time without a timepiece," Zoë said. It was as though she had her own built-in atomic clock. She always knew exactly what time it was, despite the fact that she didn't own a watch.

"I took it for granted and assumed that everyone knew what time it was all the time. It was just very natural to know that. And I didn't round it off. If

Zoë, a true healer.

it was 3:17; that's what I said when someone wanted to know the time. Every minute of the day, even during the night, I knew exactly what time it was."

There were other things she knew instinctively as well. When she was in the sixth grade, her teacher, Sister Margaret Patrice, used to get a bit disconcerted with her because her small hand would shoot up to answer a question before it was completely asked.

"Sister would stop at the second or third word and say in a challenging fashion 'Okay, what's the answer?' And I would tell her. One hundred percent of time I answered correctly for the question she was going to ask."

The Nightmare

Zoë occasionally receives premonitions through symbolic dreams. One such event happened in 1982 when her mother was ill.

"My mother was diagnosed as having had a gall bladder attack, so they scheduled her to go in for surgery to have it removed," she said. "Mom actually seemed quite healthy, other than the terribly upset stomach she was feeling."

In those days if you were scheduled for surgery, you were admitted into the hospital a few days in advance for testing. When her mother entered the hospital on a Saturday, she was still complaining of an upset stomach. Her surgery was scheduled for Tuesday because Monday was a holiday, Labor Day.

Zoë's mother lived in Worcester, Massachusetts, and Zoë had a home in northern New Jersey, so they kept in touch by telephone between visits. Over the weekend, Zoë called her mom in the hospital and they spoke for a while. Her mom seemed fine and in good spirits.

How old were you when you had your first psychic experience?

"I remember developing the multiplication tables, independently, a few weeks after my fourth birthday. I don't remember sharing it with others. I only used the mental exercise of the multiplication tables to help me fall asleep at night. I would remember where I had left off the previous night and start there."

—Zoë

"We had previously made arrangements that I would pick her up from the hospital and stay with her during her period of convalescence.

"On Monday morning at seven o'clock, I was still asleep and started to have a nightmare," Zoë said. "Bugs were going around in a circle and kept closing in on me in a spiral motion. For some reason I responded to this scene with a sense of intense fear and dread. When the bugs descended on me in the center of the spiral, seemingly for the kill, I screamed, waking myself and my husband at the same time." She glanced over at a clock by the bed and saw it read 7:20 a.m.

"An hour and a half later, the doctor called to say my mother had died at 7:20 a.m." She had suffered a heart attack. "Mom had been misdiagnosed, because gall bladder and heart attack symptoms can be the same, especially in women."

Despite their distance, their bond was such that Zoë had experienced her mother's departure from two hundred miles away.

The Sacred Heart

Having spent most of her childhood in a Catholic convent, Zoë can remember one of her strongest prayers had been to receive a visit from Jesus. It was not answered—at least not when she was young. She grew up, and eventually the unanswered prayer was forgotten. One day, decades later, someone she describes as "a very spiritual soul" made an appointment to see her for an energy-healing session.

On the afternoon of his appointment, the priest came to her office. One of his parishioners had recommended Zoë to him for her healing abilities. He was feeling exhausted from the responsibilities of his job and his flock and was hoping to feel revitalized.

"I'd never met him before," she said. "He was a portly, middle-aged man with sandy hair, and he was a soft-spoken, gentle soul." She only saw him once. His condition involved a temporary, work-related stress overload and could easily be treated in a single visit. While she was proceeding with the energy work, what Zoë saw next transported her back to her early years.

"He was a sincerely spiritual priest," she said. "While I was working on this very holy man, a startling image appeared to me, right out of my prayers from childhood. Projecting out from his heart chakra was the face of Jesus." Zoë explained that the heart chakra is a spinning vortex of energy on the spine, located at about heart level, that receives energy from the universe.

"We associate the heart chakra with love. When we feel that emotion, we experience it very strongly in the heart," she said. "When we pray, we're in a heartfelt place. I think that the universe may have used this man's pure heart as a vehicle to show me a sacred image when the time was right. My initial reaction was 'Oh, Lord, what took you so long?' Then I thought, 'Thank you for answering my childhood prayer.' Later I realized, the little girl who prayed to see the image of Jesus was not ready to have that prayer answered. It only could occur later in life when I became more deeply spiritual. I had to earn the privilege of a visit."

The message Zoë took from the experience was "You're making progress, keep it up."

Descriptions of Mystical Experiences

In the 1970s study discussed earlier in which 1,500 people were interviewed about their basic belief systems, respondents described mystical experiences as imparting the following:

A feeling of deep and profound peace	55%
A certainty that all things would work out for the good	48%
A sense of my own need to contribute to others	43%
A conviction that love is at the center of everything	43%
A sense of joy and laughter	43%
An experience of great emotional intensity	38%
A great increase in my understanding and knowledge	32%
A sense of the unity of everything and my own part in it	29%
A sense of new life or living in a new world	27%
A confidence in my own personal survival	27%

Life Force

Energy is not just a concept but a dynamic life force that can move between living creatures. This story illustrates that point.

Zoë is a cat lover and has had many beloved felines in her home over the years. She also has the ability to nonverbally communicate with them. One of her four-legged family members was named Katrina. She was a white cat with orange and black spots and a gentle, loving personality. One of the most difficult trials that any pet lover faces is when their pet becomes elderly and advances toward the end of his or her life.

"Katrina was getting weak and wasn't doing very well," Zoë said. "She slept a good bit, and this particular day she was in the far corner of the living room, curled up. I came out of the bedroom and into the hallway and peeked over there to make sure she was breathing. I saw no movement. My mind and heart started silently screaming, 'Trina! Are you okay?'" Trina woke, picked up her head, and turned it in Zoë's direction, so she could hear her faint mew. Then she put her head down and fell back to sleep.

"At a psychic level, I had asked if she was okay, and at physical level, Trina responded, 'Yes. I haven't left you yet, Mama.'"

Eventually, Katrina drew near to the end of life.

"I didn't know how close she was to death that night, but I knew it was imminent," Zoë said. "At ten o'clock, a few minutes before she passed, Trina sent her energy to me. I could see it coming toward me, and I breathed it into my chest; it permeated my lungs, heart, and upper torso. At some point I mentally said, 'Don't send me everything; save some for yourself.' The energy flow stopped immediately. Trina died shortly thereafter. I felt her energy in my chest for several months. I believe she knew that she was going in a few minutes, and she wanted to leave as much of herself with me as she could."

How has your unfolding psychic ability affected the way you treat other people, both those you know and strangers?

"Actually seeing the knife wound from a previous lifetime in someone's back gave me the gift of understanding that other people's reality and my own, while different, are equally real."

—Zoë

This sort of transfer of energy sounds strange to most people, but Zoë explains it this way: "We transfer energy all the time. We're a product of our genome, our culture, everything, and everyone. We're not isolated in any way. Even people who think they're isolated are as much a part of the whole as everyone else." She cites the story of a yogi, who, while lecturing devotees, interrupted himself with, "Oh, I'm burning in the ocean liner." He could feel and see a ship getting bombed somewhere in the world at the time it actually occurred.

"I believe Katrina wanted to help me with what she knew would be my deep grief. She was just giving of herself, transferring her energy to me to help soften my grief over her loss."

Back-Stabbing Epiphany

Every so often, Zoë finds that new areas of awareness open up for her that change the way she views the world. One such epiphany occurred at a training class she attended early in her career, when she was learning additional healing techniques.

During a Reiki meditation class, a classmate told Zoë that she knew how she had been killed in a previous life; she had been stabbed in the back. This story startled Zoë, who had never heard anyone make such a claim before.

"Well, I thought that was ridiculous," Zoë said. At the time reincarnation was a bit alien to her Catholic sensibilities. "Then she turned around, and I said, 'Let me see if I can feel it.' Not only could I feel the knife wound in her energy field, but I could see it. There was a deep gash in her back, not bleeding, just an image." This event taught Zoë to be open-minded when others made statements that reached beyond her personal experiences.

The Good Neighbor

Sometimes the directions we receive in life come from the most mysterious sources.

One afternoon Zoë was driving alone in an unfamiliar neighborhood, making a house call to one of her clients.

"It was a beautiful day," she said. "I was looking for an address. It was in a nice neighborhood with a wide, winding street and lovely houses set way back. Each house had about three acres of property. The trees were tall and older, so the foliage was up high. The properties were landscaped, and there was no fencing. I could see, from where I sat in the car, 360 degrees around me."

Unfortunately, the expansive view did not help her much. She was still lost.

Zoë spotted a man with a swarthy complexion and dark eyes by the side of the road and pulled over to ask directions.

"I rolled down my window and asked him if he knew where such-and-such street was. He directed me to where it was, and I thanked him. As I was pulling away, I looked in my rearview mirror to see what house he was going to go into. He wasn't there." She looked in all directions around her, but he had vanished.

"There was nowhere he could have gone in that space of time that I wouldn't have seen him. The man just disappeared." He had certainly shown he was a good neighbor, even if his address was on the other side.

John, Owner of a Design Agency

John and I met many years ago when we both worked at a large advertising agency in northern New Jersey. Today he owns a design agency in Morris County, New Jersey. He first realized that he might be psychic when his adoptive father was in the hospital.

Future Legacy

Throughout the ages, fathers have passed insights down to their sons. But the information John's father chose to share with him took him by surprise.

"My father was first in the hospital for bronchitis, and then he went home," John said. "Eventually, he returned to the hospital for tests on Memorial Day weekend." His father still had respiratory problems, and having recovered from a previous bout of pneumonia, his voice was a bit gravelly.

How old were you when you had your first psychic experience?

"I was twenty-four years old when I first became aware of having psychic ability. I kept it to myself, at first, because it happened when my father was about to die. There were so many emotional things going on that it was the furthest thing from my mind."

—John

"He hated hospitals," John said. "He went in on a Thursday, and I saw him on Friday." John's father wanted to hear all about his son's upcoming holiday weekend at the Jersey Shore, and he said he hoped John would meet some girls. Then he said something strange to John.

"He told me about my abilities," John said. "He spoke to me as if someone else was telling him something and he was passing it along. He said, 'You have the ability to walk into a room knowing nobody and walk out knowing everybody. You can make bonds with the good people.' But he never saw me do that. That phase of my life hadn't yet begun. He said he admired me for those abilities, and that always stuck with me." The two talked quite a while and healed whatever rifts had existed between them in the past.

John decided to cancel his plans to stay at the shore that weekend, but he didn't know why. Then he called an ex-girlfriend out of the blue. Again, he didn't know why. When he spoke to her, the normally laid-back John became so agitated that she cancelled her plans for that weekend to be with him.

"If I'm emotional, you better start listening to me; something's wrong."

John stayed with his ex-girlfriend that night.

"I knew something would happen. The next day my father found out he had lung cancer. He told me to go get his parents because he was checking out. I did, and he died that day." John was now aware that he had psychic ability, but because it occurred during such a sad event in his life, it only made him feel confused.

"Why did I contact my ex-girlfriend? I guess I knew I would need someone with me." And he was right. It was a nightmarish weekend for him. Thankfully, his intuition supplied him with the support he needed.

"She was by my side for the whole thing."

Psychic Tuner

John finds that the closer he becomes to someone, the more tuned in he becomes to their energy—and at times it can be extremely disconcerting.

When John was growing up, he had a friend Greg, who lived next door. When they were eight, Greg moved to another town about twenty miles away. Not very far by adult standards, but for a child, the move might as well have been to China. They lost contact.

Moving ahead a few decades, John befriended a man named David. David's business partner turned out to be John's childhood friend Greg. An even stranger coincidence was that when Greg had moved away from John's neighborhood so many years before, his new next-door neighbor turned out to be David. The three of them, now adults, saw each other from time to time at sports events.

David was a soft-spoken man whom John described as having had a lumberjack physique.

"David was the type of guy everyone remembered, even if you encountered him for only three minutes, years ago," John said. "He had that type of magnetic personality. Everybody liked him. You never heard a bad word about him." Eventually, John and David developed a close friendship.

"He opened up and told me everything about himself," John said. "Although everybody knew him, he never shared who he really was with anybody." Having formed this bond, John became very sensitive to David's energy.

One day John was spending some time with Greg, and he suddenly felt compelled to ask him about how David was doing. Had Greg heard from David recently? David was in good health, so the question seemed odd, even to John.

When you discovered your psychic ability, how did it alter the way you thought about the world around you?

"I'd seen him a week prior," John said. But suddenly he felt an urgent concern about David and became so annoyingly adamant about it that Greg was almost irritated in response.

"I had become close to David in the past six months, so I knew that something was wrong. 'Where is he? Call him!' I insisted. I know I was freaking Greg out. A couple minutes later, Greg received a phone call that David was in the hospital, but he didn't tell me." Greg didn't mention

"I think that things happen for a reason. It's usually a learning experience or an exit from something else. You may not know what that reason is now, but when you look back on it years from now, you'll know."

—John

the call, John said, because "he saw how frightened and upset I was, and he didn't want to upset me even more. He also didn't want what I was saying to be true. In retrospect, I'm glad that at least, in a way, I prepared him for what was to come."

Still unaware that David was sick, John couldn't sleep that night. He was agitated until about one thirty in the morning, and then suddenly calmed down and was able to doze off.

"The next morning I woke up in a panic and texted Greg. I found out that David had died about one thirty that morning of an aortic embolism. It's strange," John said, "but David had opened up to me as if he knew he was going to die."

Space Invader

John once had a ghostly encounter that gave new meaning to the concept of invading someone else's personal space.

Many years ago he was dating a woman from art school who invited him to stay at her house in Upstate New York. She and her mother lived in an old building from the 1800s that John believed might have been the servants' quarters for a large estate. Although he thought he was the sole visitor that night, he soon found out that wasn't the case.

John, his girlfriend, and her mother spent a pleasant evening socializing, which included being introduced to the family's two German shepherds. They were fairly quiet dogs who spent most of the evening resting peacefully in the room. Eventually, John retired to a guest room on the first floor. Sometime during the early hours of the morning, he experienced something odd.

"I felt something go through me," he said. "Just at the moment it that happened, the two German shepherds woke up and began barking uncontrollably. They sensed something, too, and followed it into the living room, where they paced around for some time."

John wasn't sure what to make of it. It was the middle of the night, so he didn't want to wake anyone. Instead, he waited until morning to relate his experience to his girlfriend and her mother.

Rather than being alarmed, they calmly informed him that a woman had died in the house some years before and would sometimes wake them, too, in the early hours of the morning. It was nothing to be concerned about.

"The family accepted that she was there," he said. Apparently, they viewed her as a somewhat quirky extension of the household.

Standing Room Only

For most of us, when we visit a quiet cemetery, it can impart an eerie sense of desolation. But for those who are psychic, the experience can be quite different.

Because his father died when he was in his early twenties, John didn't have many meaningful conversations with him while he was alive. Now that John is older, he often talks to his father. He passes the cemetery every day when he goes to work. Two to three times a year, he visits his father's grave. John's father is buried in St Vincent's Cemetery in Madison, New Jersey.

"It's a small, sloping cemetery in the middle of nowhere," John said. "It's very old with graves dating back to the mid-1800s. Many of my family's ancestors are buried there." No plots are left at this point; the cemetery is completely filled with graves crowding every section.

"The last time I visited my father's grave was this past Father's Day," John said. "I thought, 'I'll visit my father's grave and I'll talk to him.'" But when he got there, he found it very difficult to focus on a conversation.

"When I visit my father's grave, I feel like I'm being interrupted. I'm overwhelmed. It's like trying to have a conversation in a crowded bar. Graveyards are like a city to me." He said he can talk to his father wherever he is, and often does, so sometimes it's just better not to visit the cemetery.

Repeatability Need Not Apply

Anyone involved with science knows that scientific fact is based on experiments that can be reproduced. Dr. Irvin L. Child, Professor of Psychology at Yale University, observed in a paper presented to the American Society for Psychical Research in 1974 that "unlike other areas of experimental study, paranormal phenomena have never been the subject of any kind of dependably repeatable experiment ... Psi phenomena may, of course, be of such a nature that no procedure will ever be adequate to guarantee their occurrence at a particular time and place." Indeed, paranormal events do tend to be anecdotal by nature, so his point is well taken.

Fate Expectations

John knows many things that perhaps he shouldn't. He offered so many examples that I made a list of them.

- "I'll ask someone, 'How long has your grandmother been dead?' and they'll tell me, 'She's not dead.' But she dies within a week of my asking."

- "I'll be in a meeting, a name will pop into my head, and I'll blurt out the name. Suddenly, that person calls me or walks into the room."

- "If I'm traveling somewhere, I may suddenly take a new route and then find out I avoided a big accident that occurred on my normal route."

- "I see people's faces, and I will swear I know them even though we've never met before. I can tell them about themselves, things I don't even know: their birthday within a week, how many siblings they have, the last relationship they were in, what they do for a living, and what they are interested in. I can read their state of mind."

- "I can tell by looking at a baby picture what his or her personality is going to be like when they grow up."

- John was adopted. No one told him anything about his birth parents during his childhood. "I always knew when I was growing up that I was half Italian, half Irish." When he finally researched his birth parents as an adult, he found this to be true.

- When he receives an invitation to bid on a job for his design business, he quickly jumps on the ones he knows will come to pass. If the project has no future, he ignores it. "Someone can call me and I won't bother with the project because I know it will fall through, so I don't even write up a quote."

Marcia, Writer, Scholar, Occasional Stand-up Comedienne

I met Marcia at the same advertising agency as John. She is an extremely talented writer, a walking fount of esoteric knowledge, and one of the funniest women I've ever met. She briefly performed as a stand-up comedienne at a club in New York City.

What's Cooking?

Sometimes a psychic experience gets dismissed because it is too outlandish to believe. But when others collaborate what has been seen, the event takes on an entirely different dimension in reality. So it was with Marcia and a ghostly encounter she had.

It was the early 1990s. Marcia had never had any psychic experiences.

"I'm not particularly sensitive in that way," she said. "But something kind of strange happened. I've tried to explain it away, but I can't."

Marcia, whose smile lights up any room she enters

She moved into an efficiency apartment in an old building in Madison, New Jersey, that had been built around 1920.

"It's a very special building, because the apartments were a part of an era when well-to-do people lived in single dwellings with their families, as well as with maids and butlers," she said. "They're very large apartments with big living spaces." Her apartment had been divided off from a larger apartment on the first floor.

"It was cute," she said. "It was probably a maid's quarters at one time." The dwelling was located in a quiet neighborhood in a typical New Jersey suburb. It was a pleasantly uneventful place to call home.

Then, one very normal weeknight, something not so normal occurred.

"It was very quiet. I got into my bed," she said. "I was relaxing and about to drift off to sleep. As I was lying there, I happened to glance at the corner of the bedroom to the left of me. There was a closet and a little foyer leading out to the living room. Suddenly, I saw this image of a little woman, short and rather round. I could see her perfectly. She was wearing a snow-white apron and a dress and had black hair tied into a bun. She was holding something, but I couldn't see what it was." Marcia said she felt startled, but in her relaxed state, she was not afraid at all.

"She was very benign and sweet," Marcia said. "She was looking at me. I didn't know whether it was a near-sleep experience or something paranormal."

A few weeks later, Marcia was chatting with a neighbor and told her about the experience.

"I told her I hoped she didn't think I was crazy," Marcia said. She described her experience to the neighbor. However,

How old were you when you had your first psychic experience?

"I was already in my thirties. I shared it with my neighbor. I thought I was going a little nuts seeing that ghost, and I just wanted to share that. And then to find out that she had seen the same woman, and to have that story gel—well, naturally I was pretty taken aback. One could say, 'I saw this ghost, but it was a dream image because I was falling asleep,' but when my neighbor was able to supply details that I didn't tell her … well, that changed everything."
—Marcia

before she could finish, her neighbor said, "Oh, my God, I've seen her too!" She described the same ghostly woman perfectly.

"My neighbor chimed in that she looked like a pastry chef or baker. I said she was holding something but I couldn't quite tell what it was. Without hesitation, my neighbor told me: 'It's a rolling pin.'"

Several weeks later, Marcia asked the superintendent about who had lived in the apartment in the past.

"He said, 'About fifteen years ago, your apartment was part of a larger unit. The woman who lived in it was a baker, and the smell of her baking used to waft through the building. She passed away a couple of years ago.'"

Having her experience affirmed by her neighbor, as well as the information her superintendent supplied, astonished Marcia. She decided that she liked her new ghostly roommate.

"She reassured me. It was nice having her there."

Daphne, Administrative Assistant (Retired)

Stephen and I met Daphne and her husband, Les, on a transatlantic cruise in September of 2011. We were seated at the same dinner table every night and developed a friendship. Here are some of her remarkable stories.

The Telltale Glass

People are often warned to stay away from Ouija boards because they can be a conduit for negative energy from the other side. Sometimes it takes an unpleasant incident for the curious to learn this.

Daphne was in her midteens when she encountered her first psychic experience. She was at

Daphne, our friend who hails from the United Kingdom.

her best friend's house in Northwest London. They set up a table in the living room with a homemade Ouija board, replete with hand-drawn letters, in hopes of receiving a message from beyond. Her friend took a glass from the nearby cupboard and placed it upside down on the board.

"At first nothing much happened," she said. "It started out boring. Then the glass started moving on its own, and we became frightened." Both swore they were not moving the glass, but it glided very swiftly across the board. Daphne did not remember what messages, if any, they received. She only recalled that they stopped immediately and put the glass securely back in the cupboard.

"We were very amateurish," she said, chuckling.

Later that day, her friend's mother opened the cupboard, and before she could reach in, the glass they had used jumped up out of the cabinet on its own and bounced onto the carpet.

"We both got the significance of that," Daphne said. "We were affected by it. We knew something really happened."

Ouija Boards

Psychic medium Echo Bodine has observed that some earthbound spirits have chosen not to go to the other side. She said while they may not be evil, they can be self-centered and immature, using the living as a form of entertainment. Perhaps that's why Ouija boards, which may open a portal for these types of spirits, are generally not recommended as a constructive way to contact the departed.

Portents Not Taken

Now and then, Daphne gets strong feelings about situations, and if she doesn't follow her intuition, bad things can happen.

In England, as in the United States, one rite of passage in youth is learning how to drive a car. When Daphne was in her twenties, a friend decided that it was time for her to learn. He suggested they get together for some driving lessons in the countryside, and she instantly got a bad feeling about it.

"I just didn't want to do it," said Daphne. "I made every excuse I could think of, from not having the right shoes to saying it wasn't a convenient time." But her friend insisted, so off they went in his blue Hillman-Hunter,

How old were you when you had your first psychic experience?

"I grew up with a mother who kept saying, 'I'm having one of my feelings; be careful when you go out.' I think I was about fourteen when I first became aware of psychic experiences. My friend and I had created our own Ouija board."

—Daphne

a compact car popular in the United Kingdom in the late 1960s and 1970s.

"I felt like he had forced me to do it," she said. They were soon out driving in the country and came to a cattle grid gate that spanned the road.

"He was too lazy to get out and open the gate for the car," she said. Instead, he was adamant that she drive around the gate, through a small space between the gate and a stone wall. Unfortunately, the space was so narrow that it would have been challenging for an experienced driver, let alone a beginner.

"We smashed the car against the wall," she said. First, Daphne introduced one side of the car to the wall, and then her copilot grabbed the wheel and dented the other side of the car in an ill-fated attempt to avoid further damage. That concluded the driving lessons for the day.

Another time Daphne ignored her sixth sense, and it resulted in more serious consequences. It was years later, and she and her husband, Les, were planning a Sunday afternoon outing.

"We like to get out on a Sunday," she said. Les suggested that this time they visit a nearby mansion. Suddenly, Daphne got an overwhelming feeling that the mansion was a bad idea, but she ignored her intuition and off they went.

"We pulled up to turn right into the stately home, and a young girl in a red Peugeot smacked into the back of us. She didn't realize we were stationary." Not only was the back of their car badly damaged, but Les received neck injuries that eventually required several surgeries.

"That accident had implications for the rest our lives. I wished that I had listened to that overwhelming feeling of not wanting to go."

Daphne has no control over when she receives her premonitions. When she was working as an administrative assistant for the Meat and Livestock Commission, she had a supervisor who tended to be moody.

"He was one of those blokes who would come in all sweetness and light one day, and then the next day be miserable," she said. As a result, she didn't speak very freely with him. She just kept to her job.

So one evening, when she got a very strong feeling that her supervisor shouldn't go home, she wanted to stop him from leaving. However, Daphne didn't feel comfortable enough to share that with him.

"I felt like telling him, 'Don't go! Don't go home!' I knew something was going to happen," she said. "The next day he came in and said he had had an automobile accident." Perhaps it was karmic—had he been a more pleasant supervisor, she would have tipped him off and he might have averted his injuries altogether.

Sometimes the events Daphne foresees have more to do with life decisions than with accidents, but they can be just as hard to avoid.

"Les was very unhappy in a job he had," Daphne said. Her husband worked as an information technologies manager. He had been looking for another position, and when the first opportunity came up, he was so desperate to leave his job that he didn't give the offer due consideration.

"Another time he wouldn't have taken it, because it was so far from where we lived," Daphne said. "I had this dreadful, dreadful feeling about it." Unfortunately, her intuition ended up being right. His new supervisor treated him very badly, and the job entailed a great deal of long-distance travel.

"I just had this awful feeling when he told me he had accepted it—that it really was a mistake. He only stayed there about three months." The moral of the story: when intuition speaks, listen.

When you discovered your psychic ability, how did it alter the way you thought about the world around you?

"I think it confirmed what I always thought: that there was more going on than what you see on a day-to-day basis. There's another dimension, at least ... maybe many, many dimensions."

—Daphne

Room Service

It's often said that service isn't what it used to be, but examples can still be found of hospitality employees who go above and "beyond" in their attention to customers. This story is one of them.

Daphne and Les were staying at a Victorian hotel in Bath, England. Bath is best known for its natural hot springs that have attracted visitors for centuries as far back as the ancient Romans around 50 AD.

"We only stayed there one night," she said. "It was an old hotel. I went to bed, fell asleep, and woke up in the early morning." What she saw when she opened her eyes startled her.

"A figure was standing next to the bed, dressed in a maid uniform, holding a towel over her arm, and looking down at me. She was fortyish in age." Daphne switched the lights on and the woman vanished.

"I left that light on," she said. "I remember thinking it was a kind way that she was looking at me, like a mother looking at a child. But I didn't like seeing somebody in my room that shouldn't be there. I swear I wasn't dreaming. I know what I saw, and I definitely saw that woman."

Certainly, no one could fault the maid for her dedication to duty.

CHAPTER 8

PLAYING DEAD AND OTHER TALES

The eyes only see what they are prepared to comprehend.
— Henri Bergson, French philosopher (1859–1941)

Denise, Middle-School Teacher

Playing Dead

Children have an uncanny way of finding and making friends wherever they go, but when Denise was a youngster that natural ability went well beyond the norm.

Denise has been psychic as long as she can remember. As a child, she used to hear choruses of whispers and feel people sitting on her bed at night.

"They were so loud it would wake me up," she said. She could never understand their conversations because there were so many voices talking at once.

"I was scared of it, but my grandmother told me it was a gift from God," she said. Even as a small child, she felt a deep connection to God and felt protected. Sometimes she felt the presence of angels as well.

From the ages of five to fourteen, Denise lived across the street from a graveyard and often played there.

How old were you when you had your first psychic experience?

"Maybe I was four or five from what I remember. When I played in the graveyard, that's when it really picked up."
— Denise

"I would sit up in a tree and watch people get buried. I could feel them there."

Sometimes she would talk to the deceased inhabitants.

"I used to talk to a child there who had died in a fire. I remember her saying that she missed her mother. We'd play hide-and-seek in the graveyard. I found out years later, as an adult, that there was a family buried there—a father, six children, and a grandmother—and everyone had died in a fire except the mother."

Missing Jewelry

Even grandmothers have mothers who watch over them from the other side. It would seem that maternal instinct never dies.

When Denise was fourteen, she went to bed one night and received an unexpected visitor in her dreams. Her great-grandmother Florence, whom she had never met in life, came to chat with her.

Denise's grandmother Francis had lost a ring that was important to her because it had sentimental value, and she was very upset. She didn't own very much jewelry, but this ring had the birthstones of all of her children in it. Great-Grandmother Florence decided to help out in the matter and told Denise where the ring was.

"I remember telling my grandmother that her jewelry was behind the dresser," Denise said. "She responded by asking, 'Who told you?' 'Your mother told me,' I said."

Her grandmother moved the dresser away from the wall, and to her surprise, the ring was there. She was extremely grateful to Denise and Florence for helping her to find her precious heirloom.

Medical Messages

Psychic special deliveries can arrive at the most peculiar times.

"I can't plan getting messages. I can't do readings," Denise said. Instead, the messages seem to find her.

"One time I was in the grocery store and got a message from a woman's recently deceased aunt to pass on to her," she said.

Denise was looking at greeting cards, and she turned to a woman next to her and blurted out, "I want you to know that there's a woman in the hospital that you know who is pregnant, and she's going to be all right." She added, "The woman started to cry, and I cried too."

Another time Denise had a close friend with whom she worked who'd had a miscarriage.

"She was pregnant again. I suddenly turned to her and said, 'Your progesterone level is too low. Unless you start supplements today, you're going to lose the baby.'" The woman rushed to her doctor, and he confirmed that she did, indeed, need those supplements. Denise said that her friend carried the pregnancy to term and had a healthy baby girl.

Dark Energy

Denise said that sometimes energy can be so toxic that she has to get away from it.

Once she visited some brick buildings on the former site of a New Jersey state mental institution that were converted to offices. What she felt there was very uncomfortable.

How has your psychic ability affected the way you treat other people, both those you know and strangers?

"It has absolutely affected the way I deal with people, because I am so sensitive and intuitive. I have a good rapport with my students ... I can feel intuitively that some people have a lot going on emotionally, so I always try to make them feel good."
—Denise

"I went into the building to visit a nonprofit organization," she said. "The woman I was supposed to talk with was on the phone, so I was waiting. Every hair on my neck was standing up. I had to get out of there. This place was demonic." She soon found out that the man who had previously lived and worked there was a doctor who had betrayed the trust of his pediatric patients by sexually abusing them.

"The energy in there was extremely dark," Denise said. She explains that when

you encounter that type of negative energy, it elicits a fight-or-flight response. "You know you can't fight it, so it is better to just get away. It's too strong to take on; it'll make you sick."

Mortality Check

Sometimes when people die, they're unaware that they're dead, or so say many books written by mediums. Apparently, the departed often don't feel any differently when they leave their bodies, so death can be confusing. When they fall into this disoriented state, sometimes the only person they can talk to—and actually are drawn to—is a medium. Denise has been the recipient of many such visits, but she remembers one in particular that truly touched her heart.

"A couple of years ago, I was sleeping and I had a visitor. A police officer came to me, lay down on the bed, and held my hand. 'Did I die?' he asked. I told him he had," she said. "'I don't want to leave my wife,' he said. I told him he needed to go to the light. It was so real that when I woke up, I wondered if my brother who is a police officer had died." She rarely hears from her brother, but as if to reassure her that all was well, he called to talk to her that morning. He didn't really have much to say, oddly enough.

"I was stunned to get his phone call," she said. It would have been great to share her previous night's experience with him, but her brother doesn't believe in the paranormal. So when they spoke, she never mentioned the visit from his departed comrade in blue.

She added, however, that she will never forget the man's obvious love for his wife and his heart-tugging reluctance to leave her behind.

Final Call

People often report getting mysterious phone calls after a loved one dies. Most of the time they report hearing static, or nothing at all, at the other end of the line. That can leave room for doubt about whether their loved one actually called or their phone was simply malfunctioning.

Where do you think your psychic ability comes from?

"I really think a lot of it is in my blood. My grandmother was extremely psychic. I was exposed to it when I was very young."
—Denise

Denise's phone line apparently has better reception.

Her grandparents lived with her most of her life, and she was very close to them. Her grandmother was very soft-spoken and gentle.

"My grandfather was 100 percent Irish, born on St. Patrick's Day," she said. "He was always encouraging me and telling me how special I was. He was a really good man."

On the evening her grandfather died, in the middle of the night the phone rang and he was at the other end. He said, "Hi, it's Grandpa. I died and I wanted to say good-bye." When Denise told her cousin about it the next day, Denise was in for another surprise. Her cousin said she had received the same farewell call from him.

Long Distance
Why would the dead call? This question is raised in the book *Phone Calls from the Dead*, by paranormal investigators D. Scott Rogo and Raymond Bayless. If someone is not psychic enough to receive messages in other ways, a call may be the best option. It takes no special paranormal ability to hear a voice on a phone line. Longing for contact with dead loved ones is a common human desire. Perhaps friends and relatives on the other side feel the same way.

Tides of Reassurance

There are many ways loved ones on the other side can communicate with those they have left behind. If one looks and listens, a message often comes.

When Denise's grandfather died in 1988, it left a void in her life. Every so often memories of him would randomly cross her mind. Months passed, and one summer day, she and some girlfriends went to Point Pleasant at the Jersey Shore to relax. It was a perfect day at the beach; the sun was shining, the ocean breezes kept the heat from being stifling, and the sounds of the waves lapping on the sand had an almost hypnotic effect. For some reason Denise's mind drifted to her grandfather, and she wondered how he was doing on the other side.

"Water calms and soothes me," Denise said. "I like to stand where the waves wash up on the shore and collect shells and pick up rocks. All of a sudden I felt something hit my foot. I looked down, and there was a five-inch, metal Celtic cross washing in on the waves. I knew it was from him." Having received his message loud and clear, she picked up the cross and threw it back into the ocean. He had not forgotten her. She had all the reassurance she needed.

Butterfly Souls

Denise said the spiritual world is constantly sending her visual symbols, but she doesn't always know right away what they mean.

She was at a girlfriend's house one day. Her friend was having a hard time with many things in her life, and Denise was there to offer support.

"I saw a butterfly land near her, struggling to fly," she said. "Finally, it turned over and died. I researched the symbol of a dying butterfly and found that in the Hopi Indian culture, when a butterfly dies near someone, it means that the soul of a dead child is watching over them. What I didn't know was that she had suffered a miscarriage. When I told her about the symbol, that's when she shared that with me. She was really scared about her marriage falling apart. At least now she had the comfort of knowing that the soul of the child she lost was protecting her."

Symbols from Beyond

One of the most common ways the dead communicate with those they leave behind is through symbols, according to paranormal researchers Bill and Judy Guggenheim. Sometimes symbols just appear and other times they are in response to a prayer for a sign. The Guggenheims found that the most common symbols included butterflies, rainbows, flowers, various species of birds, and other animals.

Norah, Owner of a Public Relations Firm

Coming of Sage

When Norah decided to visit a psychic many years ago, she thought she might learn something interesting, but the message he delivered fell squarely into the realm of the unexpected.

"I had heard about this man through word of mouth," she said. "He also had a column in the *New York Post*. I heard he was good, and I decided it would be fun."

His home, where he did the readings, was in lower Manhattan. She made an appointment for midday Saturday. The time came and she found herself standing in front of a brownstone building. The wood door had a heavy, black iron knocker that made an impressive sound when she banged it.

A short, bald man with dark eyes and a serious expression opened the door.

"What are you doing here?" he asked, almost in irritation. She told him she was there for a reading.

"You could read me," he replied and proceeded to inform her that she was probably more psychic than he was.

"So you think I'm psychic?" she asked, startled.

"Absolutely," he replied.

While she doesn't remember most of the information he related to her that day, she has never forgotten being told of her preternatural abilities.

"I always thought I was a bit psychic, but I think he validated it," she said.

Psychic Opinions

When psychic information softens troubling news, it can be a blessing.

One afternoon when Norah was working in her public relations office, she received an overseas call from her father-in-law, Harry. He was calling from his native England to share some bad news.

How old were you when you had your first psychic experience?

"I guess I was eighteen. All of a sudden I woke up one morning and knew I was moving to New York City. I lived in Ottawa, Canada, at the time. I told everyone I was moving to New York City in two months. They tried to talk me out of it, but eventually they were excited for me."
—Norah

"Harry is straight to the point when he talks," Norah said. And what he had to say set her back in her chair.

"A doctor had told him he had a spot on his lung and he had eighteen months to live," she said. "I said, 'Absolutely not,' and set him up with another doctor." She blurted out her unofficial second opinion without thinking, but she was convinced she was right.

Harry was in his sixties but still worked as a general contractor overseeing construction projects. The tall Englishman was very active and in great shape.

"The moral of the story is I was 100 percent right," she said. It turned out that the black spot on his x-ray was a normal occurrence that often happens when someone has a cold. It was not cancer—a source of relief to both Harry and his wife.

"They were happy to find that out, although I don't think they put much stock in my prediction," she said. This event happened two years ago. Harry remains active and well.

She received slightly more credit for her psychic prognosis when a close friend's husband, Robin, was diagnosed with prostate cancer. His prognosis wasn't good. The doctor had told him that he had complications and didn't offer much hope.

Norah waited until she saw them in person at a charity event to tell them that she disagreed with what the doctor had said.

"I just blurted it out," she said. It was the night before he was to take a test to confirm the diagnosis. Norah told them she was confident that Robin was well. While this was nice to hear, they still didn't believe her until his test results came back. "I think he wanted to believe me," she said.

A week later the results confirmed what she had known all along: Robin was fine.

"He was happy about it," she said. "He said, 'Yeah, you were right.'"

It was a double bonus. She not only had a clean bill of health for her friend's husband, but also for the state of her psychic abilities. Both were alive and well.

Lori, Corporate Safety Specialist

Soul Mates

Some people are destined to be together, regardless of what their future may hold.

"Mark and I started dating when we were fourteen," said Lori. She had met him in their high school art class, and they quickly became best friends. Mark had long red hair, sparkling blue eyes, and was usually dressed in the hallmark '70s disco tight jeans, silk shirt, and boots. Lori was a petite blond with an infectious smile. Their hometown of Jackson, New Jersey, was a rural area at that time.

"We were together on and off during our school years," she said.

"We both decided we were the best of friends, and so we had other relationships. He was easygoing, very dependable, and caring. He played the guitar beautifully and could always make me laugh."

When they graduated from college, Mark asked Lori to marry him and she said yes. They started a life together and eventually had two children, a boy and a girl. Little did Lori know that a dark cloud would later descend on their marriage.

Mark began drinking. As the years went by, his drinking gradually took over their lives. Eventually, they both had to face the painful fact that he was an alcoholic. Lori felt she had no choice but to legally separate from her husband. A year and a half later, Mark returned to her and said he was changing his ways and going to Alcoholics Anonymous.

"He came back and told me that I was the only woman he had ever loved, and he was getting his act together," she said. "I told him he'd have to prove it first before we got back together." He promised he would and returned to South Carolina, where he worked as a general contractor.

It was a turning point in their relationship, and Lori felt a sense of hope about their future. Two weeks passed. Then came the phone call. Mark's next-door neighbor in South Carolina contacted Lori, and he had some difficult news to share.

How old were you when you had your first psychic experience?

"I was fifteen. I was on the phone with my boyfriend, Mark, and we were arguing about something. I was just furious with him about his smoking. On his end of the line, he turned around and an ashtray came flying at him. It was the first time I started to realize that something was really different about me."

—Lori

"Mark had died of a heart attack," Lori said. When she traveled to collect his body for the funeral, she found the Alcoholics Anonymous paperwork among his effects and knew that he had kept his word.

"He was buried on Saturday, and I stayed at his mother's house that night," she said. When she awoke the next morning, she saw a brilliant white light radiating in one corner of the bedroom.

"Suddenly this song he had always sung to me popped into my head, and I immediately understood that everything was okay." She sat up in bed, stunned but comforted. "He was saying good-bye for the last time. I knew he still loved me."

Claudia, Retired Substitute Teacher, Counselor for Children at Risk

Living in Neutral

In the right environment, natural talents can blossom. Psychic abilities are no exception.

When Claudia was thirty, she and her husband went house hunting. One unique complication they had to contend with, above and beyond what most house hunters encounter, was her sensitivity to energy. Many homes they visited, while visually pleasant, imparted an energy that made her feel uncomfortable.

"When looking at one of many lovely homes, we were told our children could attend Mountain Lakes High School," Claudia said. Mountain Lakes is a wealthy community with highly rated schools.

"I remember walking through the house. It was very old. There was something uncomfortable about it. I couldn't get through the whole house. I was beginning to feel ill. When they suggested we see the basement, I couldn't bring myself to go there. I didn't know what was in that house, but I knew I had to leave immediately. I was finished viewing homes for that day."

Finally, they found a house in a semi-rural area of Rockaway Township, New Jersey. Across the street was land owned by conservancies for wildlife preservation. She knew it would work because the energy there was neutral.

"I could put a mark on it," she said. "It could be part of me." It was a bi-level home built on what once was an old sheep farm.

How old were you when you had your first psychic experience?

"I think I was in high school when I really became aware of what being psychic was all about. I know that people used to come to me when they had problems. I was the go-to person. I didn't have more knowledge; I had more compassion. I was able to see the many facets of each individual."

—Claudia

The first floor had a guest room situated three feet beneath ground level that imparted a soothing energy.

"People have visited my home at times, both the mentally and physically ill. After spending time in that room, they seemed miraculously healed," she said. The house also helped clear her mind so that her psychic abilities began to grow and develop.

"The land is old and just very neutral," she said. "It opened up my mind in a way that it was never open before." From that point on, her psychic abilities began to grow.

Energetic Residue

Any object or place touched by humans will possess some energy, says psychic medium Concetta Bertoldi. More specifically, places where people have been for a long time, or where intense or highly emotional events have occurred, are imbued with corresponding human energy, such as joy, peace, grief, or fear.

Therapeutic Footing

Most people require proof to believe in psychic phenomena. And that's certainly reasonable. Claudia unwittingly supplied that proof to a stalwart skeptic.

As she entered her thirties, Claudia's psychic abilities kept increasing in intensity.

"I had this sense of knowing. I would go around almost seeing through people." Unfortunately, she sometimes knew a little too much about other people's private issues, blurting out what she knew and losing friends in the process.

"I was upset about losing a very close friend, so I went to see a therapist about it," she said. The therapist didn't take her psychic abilities seriously, instead opting to treat her problems on a more clinical level. "I said, 'You can believe me or not believe me—that's okay.' I don't think she actually believed me."

That is, until Claudia made a prediction about her therapist that came true.

"I remember one incident in particular. As was her habit, my therapist sat on a comfortable chair with a footstool at her feet. One day she informed me of her upcoming vacation to Upstate New York, and that we would have to postpone our next session. For some reason I blurted out a premonition. I said, 'The next time I see you, you're going to have your foot in a cast, propped up on your footstool. You may want to come back from your vacation early.'" The therapist smiled.

Sure enough, the next time Claudia saw her therapist, her foot was in a cast and up on the stool.

"I didn't know at the time that she had been planning on skiing that weekend," Claudia said. Just to make sure her patient's prediction wouldn't come true, the therapist stayed behind at the lodge while her family took to the slopes. Unfortunately, she tripped on a rug and broke her ankle.

"She was totally a believer after that."

Back to the Garden

When people move far from home, they can lose their way on many levels. But guides are there to help, if one is perceptive enough to see them.

Claudia's husband often worked long hours, so sometimes she and her daughter would frequent a local Asian vegetarian restaurant. The establishment offered a welcoming environment, where her daughter could work on homework and they could enjoy a relaxing dinner together. They became regular customers, and a petite Asian woman always waited on them.

How has your unfolding psychic ability affected the way you treat other people, both those you know and strangers?

"When these abilities became stronger, they began to interfere with my life. I began seriously dealing with boundary issues and became more cognizant about not invading other people's space."
—Claudia

"I felt a certain sadness deep within this lovely young woman each time we frequented the restaurant," Claudia said. "One night I decided to speak with her and asked what made her so sad." The woman politely smiled but didn't respond.

"On our next visit, the young waitress approached me and confessed she had been thinking about my question since the last time we had dined there. She told me of a place she had frequented in her childhood. Immediately, an image appeared to me. It was a beautiful garden complete with a fresh water pond. I told her, 'You don't have to describe it to me. I already know what it looks like!'" Claudia later learned that the woman had spent the better part of her childhood there and had drawn a deep sense of personal peace from the garden.

"I said, 'The place you come from is unbelievably beautiful. You haven't been able to find a spiritual place like that here in America.' Her sadness enveloped me."

Claudia suggested places in the area where the woman might find that same sense of peace and spirituality. The woman later found a Buddhist temple near where she lived in New York City.

"To go with her on this journey in her mind was the deepest I ever went into another human being," Claudia said, grateful to have helped the woman. "I remember closing my eyes and having a sense of dreaming with her. I was able to bring her back to a simpler time in her life."

Children at Risk

Children are particularly vulnerable souls, so any support they can get along the way to adulthood can make a meaningful difference in their lives.

Claudia is a licensed counselor and has spent considerable time outside her teaching job volunteering to assist children of divorce or those trying to cope with an alcoholic or drug-addicted parent. While she doesn't counsel at school, sometimes students seek her out for advice, and she will help them in any way she can.

"A young girl from the middle school often came to my room to talk," she said. "Her parents were divorced. She had to travel on weekends to see her father and was often reluctant to go. Her mother would insist on these visits nevertheless. On one occasion this girl seemed more upset than usual about her weekend journey. I sensed something really dark as she spoke. I had a strong urge to prevent her from making this particular trip. It was as if I needed to pull her back from an impending avalanche."

Claudia told the girl that it might be best to follow her instincts and not see her father. After a long conversation, she realized that nothing she said was going to prevent the visit from taking place, so she persuaded the girl to take a friend with her.

Claudia didn't know what would happen that weekend, but she knew it would be traumatic. While the event couldn't be averted, having a friend along might serve as a buffer.

"When the girl and her friend arrived at her father's apartment, they found that he had hanged himself," she said. "Thank God she was not completely alone."

Hot Tip

From time to time, images of future events appear to Claudia, but she doesn't know when or where they will occur. Although, she said they usually take place within a week.

"My friend Denise has a boyfriend who owns an auto body shop. She was talking to me about his office there when I began to get a vision," Claudia said. "While she was talking, I saw a room that looked like an office, but it had a bed in it. Then I felt a sense of urgency and saw the office engulfed in flames."

Claudia told Denise about it, but she wasn't sure if it was his office or home. Claudia suggested that her boyfriend check his place of business for fire hazards, such as unsafe electrical wiring or spilled chemicals.

Denise didn't know it at the time, but her boyfriend had a home office, with a bed in it, that was located in a shack-like building near the house he rented. She found out about it soon enough.

"The next time I heard from Denise was a week later, when she sent me a text message telling me that her boyfriend's home office had burned down." Fortunately, no one was hurt.

Maria, Domestic Artist

The Second Floor

Sometimes when people leave this world, they want to share the joy of their physical liberation with others. Such was the case with the long-infirmed Grandma Rose.

Maria and her daughter Shannon cared for Maria's grandmother Rose for the last three months of her life.

"Grandma Rose was the sweetest person in the world," Shannon said. "She never had anything bad to say about anyone, and she was always one to do charity work."

How old were you when you had your first psychic experience?

"I was forty-two. It opened up a spiritual world for me. I knew it was there. It wasn't all talk."
—Maria

Grandma Rose was ninety-eight years old when she died. Prior to that, she had been unable to climb stairs for quite some time, confining her to the ground floor of the house.

"Many spirits came by to visit her during those months we cared for her," Maria said. "She would always say, 'My mother is on my shoulder.' She named so many people that I couldn't remember them all." Apparently, her deceased family was busily planning for a reunion on the other side.

"I was holding her hand when she passed away," Maria said. "You could hear all this chatter. You could hear her mother, her father, her husband, her son. When she finally passed away, the voices were gone."

After she died, the family heard knocking sounds upstairs—part of Grandma Rose's liberation.

"She had not been able to go upstairs for several years," Maria said. For days after the funeral, they noticed activity on the second floor.

"She kept a Rottweiler at the house, and our cousin upstairs would lock her bedroom door so her cat would not encounter the dog," Maria said. "We locked the bedroom door before the funeral, and when we came back, the door was wide open. Everyone insisted they hadn't touched it." For the week following the funeral, whenever they locked the door, they would find it unlocked and open again. Fortunately, the dog never went upstairs and the cat kept to itself.

"We knew it was Grandma. She wanted everyone to know that she was finally able to go upstairs again," Maria said.

Shannon, Student, Maria's Daughter

Shannon and Maria occasionally sense the same things, but Shannon says that her abilities are stronger than her mother's and have been since she was a small child. She's now seventeen years old.

Remember Me

Sometimes all the dead want is not to be forgotten, particularly if their fate in life went undiscovered by those they loved.

Once, Shannon and Maria shared a strange sensation.

"We would smell this horrible scent, like smelling death," Shannon said. "As time went on, I began to see a black figure. All you could see was the eyes. My mother was telling me to not be scared and to ask it what it wanted."

After a while, Shannon sensed that the visitor was a girl.

"When I finally got the guts to ask what she wanted, all I could hear was a girl screaming in pain. In a couple of days, I asked her again, 'What happened?'"

The images Shannon saw took place

How old were you when you had your first psychic experience?

"I was around four years old. I saw a shadow figure of a man down the hallway near the door of one of the bedrooms. It turned out to be my great-grandpa.

I think he may have just wanted me to know who he was. He said, 'You're my great-granddaughter. I want to know you. We never got a chance to actually meet.' He had died before I was born."

—Shannon

on her property long before her house had been built. The girl's name was Lucille and she was in her teens. She was a pretty girl with curly brunette hair and wore an old-fashioned dress that went down to her knees.

"The property was all woods at that time," she said. "People were around a campfire. They tied Lucille to a chair and burned her alive. Down the road is a boulder pit. She was buried there. It happened probably in the late 1800s or early 1900s." Apparently, people had searched for Lucille, but she was never found. Shannon didn't get a sense of who the girl's attackers had been, other than a feeling that they were also young and had a common animosity toward her.

"She went away after I got that vision," Shannon said. "I think she needed to tell someone what happened to her. Sometimes they just want someone to know, to be heard."

Lake Children

Sometimes grief can last a lifetime—and beyond.

Shannon lives in a lake community in Eastern Pennsylvania.

"A couple months after Lucille, I started seeing these two little boys running around in the house, giggling." Their presence felt eerie to Shannon, although she didn't get a negative vibe from them.

"The two boys were blind. I started to see X's on their eyes—bloody X's. I asked them what happened. I got the image of boys playing around by a lake on a recreational island we have here. There were three docks on the island that were somewhat decrepit and rickety at that time. All the docks are rebuilt now."

They were brothers, and Shannon said both of them had been born blind. She saw that one of the boys had fallen into the lake and was calling for help. The older brother, Richard, was trying to find him. He could hear his younger brother screaming. He tried to help but couldn't find him. Eventually, the younger brother drowned.

"This happened probably in the mid-1950s," she said. "The older brother was about fourteen; his brother was five. The older brother felt sorrow and regret."

Eventually, she saw Richard grow older, giving her the impression that he grew up and lived a normal lifespan. Evidently, the death of his younger brother haunted him not only in life but also in death.

Pat, Retail Price Team Member

Special Valentines

Sometimes love at first sight is more than a cliché.

Richard first saw Pat in church and later told her that when he'd set his eyes on her, he thought to himself, "That's the girl I'm going to marry."

"We hadn't even met yet," Pat said. They began dating in 1970 and tied the knot in 1972. "We were soul mates," she said. They spent three happy decades together.

Sadly, in 2002 Richard developed cancer, which eventually took his life. After a decade without him, Pat still has no interest in any other man and insists she never will.

"He was a funny man, a great cook, and a very good-natured, wonderful husband," she said. To her way of thinking, there is no point in settling for less than the best, and that was Richard.

Apparently, he feels the same way about her. In 2011, on Valentine's Day, she was rummaging around in a drawer for something, feeling around with her hands, and pulled out a

Pat and Richard beaming on their wedding day.

small envelope. It was from a past bouquet Richard had given her, but she felt that finding it on Valentine's Day was no coincidence. The envelope read, "I wish I could be with you." Inside was the message, "I love you. I love you very much."

"I felt that he was reaching out to me on Valentine's Day, because I found the envelope without really looking," Pat said.

The following year on Valentine's Day, Richard sent his sweetheart another message, this time via her computer.

"I came home from work, turned on the computer, and when the screen came up for AOL, it came up with his screen

How old were you when you had your first psychic experience?

"I was thirty-four. I was sleeping with my husband when I awoke ... I saw my father. He had died in July. I always felt that it was my dad's way of saying he was going on to heaven."

—Pat

name," she said. "I have never used his screen, and I've long forgotten his password. So, I shut the computer down and started it up again to get rid of the screen, but his name came back up again."

After several tries, she eventually got in and switched names.

"I think he was just letting me know he was around and that he still cares."

Electronic Phenomena

Thomas Alva Edison, Guglielmo Marconi, and Nikola Tesla were fascinated by the prospect of electronically communicating with the dead. One of the first people to actually record such voices was Latvian-born film producer Friedrich Jurgenson. In 1959, while recording birdsongs in the woods of Sweden, he accidently captured a man's voice discussing the nocturnal habits of birds. A few weeks later, he recorded a female voice that called him by his childhood pet name, and he immediately recognized the voice as being his late mother's. He went on to record hundreds of other voices in various languages and published his findings in a 1964 book titled *Voices from the Universe.*

CHAPTER 9

PATHS OF THE PSYCHIC MASTERS

There is a theory which states that if ever anybody discovers exactly what the Universe is for and why it is here, it will instantly disappear and be replaced by something even more bizarre and inexplicable. There is another theory which states that this has already happened.
—Douglas Adams, English writer/humorist (1952–2001)

Psychic Mastery

From the many interviews conducted for this book, I have observed that psychic ability is inherent in everyone, but as pointed out earlier, certain people seem to have a more natural inclination for it than others. Many of us encounter only one or two episodes in a lifetime. Others may experience psychic phenomena quite often but have no control over when such events come to call. Then there are those special, gifted few who have a mastery over their sixth sense and are able to share it with others at will. I refer to these people as professional psychics, and this chapter highlights the experiences of four very different practitioners.

Concetta Bertoldi, Professional Psychic Medium

Home for the Holidays

Thanksgiving has a special significance in Concetta Bertoldi's family. It has been a time of both separation and reunion.

"My mother, Eleanor, was raised in an orphanage in Irvington, New Jersey, back in the 1930s," Concetta said. "It was a terrible place where she was beaten and starved. When she was six years old, they put her to work in the kitchen, cooking with pots that were bigger than she was. She often got burned, and there was no medical attention." Eleanor's

Concetta Bertoldi, a psychic medium who lives in Boonton Township, New Jersey.

mother, Helen, was still alive, but she was an alcoholic, so her daughter and three sons were placed in the orphanage.

"One day when my mother was seven, my grandmother Helen went to visit my mom and promised her that she would take her home for Thanksgiving and give her a traditional holiday meal. My mom was so excited that she waited at the end of the driveway at the orphanage all day. About four o'clock in the afternoon, an adult came out and told her, 'Your mother is dead. Come inside,' and that's how she found out her mother had died." Helen passed away at the age of twenty-seven from cirrhosis of the liver.

Concetta observes that when people are abused as children, they can react in one of two ways: either they can pass on the abuse or become very compassionate and loving. Her mother, fortunately, took the second route. Eleanor grew into a beautiful woman with reddish blonde hair, blue eyes, and a delicate porcelain complexion befitting her Irish heritage. She was married happily for fifty years and had three children—her daughter Concetta and two sons, Robert and Harold. Sadly, her son Harold and husband, Manuel, predeceased her.

"On Thanksgiving day in 2008, we

How old were you when you had your first psychic experience?

"My mother said I had them from the time I could talk. The first one I remember was when I was ten years old. I was playing with a friend at a distance from my home. We lived in a very rural area, so homes were spread far apart. Spirits told me while I was playing that I wasn't going to have my brother Harold for very long. I was only a kid, but I still knew what they meant. I ran home to find that he was okay, but I knew he would be a short-lived soul on this earth. At the age of thirty-eight, he died of AIDS."
—Concetta

invited Mom to join us at a friend's house for Thanksgiving," Concetta said. "We talked to her about it the night before to finalize times, and she was very excited about it." During the night Eleanor became ill and called the paramedics, who rushed her to the hospital.

"My brother was at her side when she passed. Shortly after, for the first and only time in my life, I heard a homecoming on the other side," Concetta said. "My mother was greeted like the guest of honor at a birthday party by everyone she had known and loved in life. I heard her embracing other souls and laughing!"

As a professional psychic medium, Concetta communicates with spirits on the other side every day, but this was a deeply emotional and personal experience for her. She reflected on the irony of her mother's death that day.

"Can you imagine? Seventy years after she had promised, my grandmother Helen finally kept her word and took my mother home for Thanksgiving."

Thomas John, Professional Psychic Medium

Vanishing Act

Thomas John was aware from early childhood that he had psychic abilities, but he didn't grow up in an environment that nurtured his gift, so it went ignored for many years. An overachiever, he attended the University of Chicago, where he triple-majored in human development, psychology, and economics. His ambition was to pursue a career in clinical psychology.

"That was my focus, and I didn't want to hear of anything else," he said. But that was not the career path he was destined to take—and

Thomas John, a psychic medium who lives in New York City.

an unlikely advisor would tap him on the shoulder to deliver that message.

Both Thomas and his sister were raised near Boston. One day they decided to go into town for some Christmas shopping. They were wandering with no particular sense of purpose down Newbury Street when they came upon a small shop featuring psychic readings. On a lark they entered.

As they crossed the threshold, a woman sitting inside greeted them. She had piercing black eyes, dark, wavy midlength hair, and a light brown complexion.

"During the psychic reading, she told me, 'You're trying to be a therapist. You're not going into therapy. You're going to be more than a therapist. You're going to do what I do,'" Thomas said.

This was not what he wanted to hear. She went on to tell him that he had psychic abilities and would be well known for them by the time he was thirty.*

How old were you when you had your first psychic experience?

"I was four years old. I saw my paternal grandfather. He told me there was a missing wristwatch that had been passed down to him from his grandfather. No one could find it after he died. I didn't even know about this. He said his best friend, Jack, had the watch. So my family went traipsing down to find my grandfather's best friend. He had the watch and gladly returned it to my father."

—Thomas

"I said, 'You're full of it,'" Thomas said.

About six years later, after her prediction came to pass, he and his sister decided to revisit the woman. If nothing else, they could at least let her know that she had, oddly enough, been right. But when they returned to the same address on Newbury Street, they found a coffee shop there instead.

"We went into the coffee shop and asked the owner where the psychic was," Thomas said. The proprietor looked a bit puzzled. "He said, 'We've been here for twenty years.'

"Both my sister and I remember the exact location of the psychic's storefront. This was

---

*He was twenty-eight when I interviewed him for this book.

where we had seen her." But according to the shop owner, no other stores had been at his location for more than two decades. The woman and the storefront they had seen, it would seem, had never existed.

Keeping in Touch

School friends often lose touch when they move along different paths in life. Such was the case with Thomas and his childhood friend Kevin. Thomas had attended college and was preparing for a career in clinical psychology. He worked at the Bipolar Research Unit at Yale University in New Haven, Connecticut. Foregoing college, Kevin had taken a job in his uncle's fish hatchery on the Boston docks. Though they had not seen each other in a while, they remained friends.

One afternoon Thomas was strolling across the New Haven Green when he saw Kevin, an imposing athletic figure at six feet, one inch. He was a welcome sight, but what was he doing so far from home?

"Vividly, as clear as day, I saw my friend," Thomas said. "He just looked at me, waved, and then he was gone." The experience startled him, so he called Kevin, but there was no answer—not unusual. His friend worked long hours, so he might not have been back from work yet. Still, Thomas had an uneasy feeling.

Thomas's mother still lived in the Boston area, so he called her. His timing was quite strange, she told him. Kevin had just been in a terrible accident, and since his family was out of town, she was on the way to the hospital to offer support. The young man had been walking alongside the road to get his mail when he was struck by a drunk driver.

She was wondering, hopefully, if Thomas had heard from him. It seemed better not to say. He had, of course, received a message from his friend, but not in the usual way.

"His spirit had come to visit me before moving on."

Passing Time

One day an elderly, well-dressed woman came to Thomas for a reading.

"She didn't have any particular goal in mind," he said. "She thought having a reading would be fun and wanted to talk to her parents." As he began the reading, he asked her if there was someone in her life named Bob, Rob, or Robert. She replied, yes, and that Rob was her husband.

"I said, 'I see him playing poker, playing the violin ... he's telling me he's sorry he passed so quickly.'"

She validated that Rob did, indeed, play poker and the violin, but then told him that her husband was not dead. In fact he was working at his dental office, taking care of some paperwork while she was having the reading, and they planned to meet for dinner afterward.

"So we skipped that part of the reading," he said; it didn't make any sense. She liked her session overall, though, and left his office quite satisfied.

"The next day the woman called me. Her husband had died of a heart attack while at his office. No one else had been there." So Rob, unfortunately, had been dead while she had her session with Thomas.

Even Thomas was surprised at how quickly her husband had come through after his death.

"It shows just how thin the veil is."

Forever Jung

Most people associate Carl Gustav Jung with the theories of the collective unconscious and archetypal symbols. Lesser known was his fascination with the paranormal, which originated with his mother Emilie's side of the family. His grandfather Reverend Samuel Preiswerk believed in spirits and kept a seat in his study for his deceased first wife, who, he said, often came to visit. The good reverend asked Jung's mother Emilie to drive away spirits who distracted him while he was working. Emilie possessed mediumistic powers and also channeled. For most of his career, Jung avoided mention of his psychic background, for fear it would hurt his credibility as a psychotherapist. However, following a near-death experience in 1944, he openly explored the paranormal world in his studies and writings.

Unwanted Message

When skeptics encounter proof of the other side, it can have a profound impact on their lives.

Recently, a couple came to see Thomas for a reading. The woman was looking forward to the experience, but her husband made it clear that he didn't believe in psychic readings and didn't want any messages.

"He was a police officer and came dressed in uniform," Thomas said. "The woman's father had passed a month earlier. She had a need to talk to him and make sure he was okay."

As the reading progressed, many things came through that the woman could validate.

Soon Thomas turned to the husband and said, "I'm getting a message for you. I'm getting, Loulou, your grandma. She says she had only one leg?" The man confirmed that this was so; she had been diabetic and had to have one of her legs amputated.

Thomas said, "She is thankful that you visit her at the cemetery every Monday morning before you go to work."

The husband was astonished at the accuracy of the message. For someone who arrived not wanting to participate, he left the office a true believer with a new perspective on the world around him.

The Neighbor

If the departed want to get through to a loved one, they will find a way.

Several years ago, before Thomas became a professional psychic, a woman named Cheryl came for a reading accompanied by her friend and neighbor, Sara. Sara sat patiently in the next room during the session.

"The first person who came through was her mom, who had died from cancer ten years before. Then I said, 'Your daughter's coming through.'" Cheryl replied that she didn't have a daughter on the other side. But Sara did, so they called her in from the waiting room.

"Her daughter had died falling out of a window," Thomas said. "It had torn the family apart. The father had divorced Sara after that." The daughter advised her mother that it was time to confront the

When you discovered your psychic ability, how did it alter the way you thought about the world around you?

"I didn't have an awareness that being psychic was something different. It altered things when I realized that a lot of people don't have this ability. I had to be careful who I talked to about it. When I began sharing it with people, I understood how careful I had to be."

—Thomas

situation, work through it, and move on. No one was to blame. Hearing from her departed daughter provided the woman with comfort and a new sense of direction in life.

"It was very life changing for her," he said.

No Place like Home

Anyone who has a psychic family member understands the importance of heeding premonitions. A woman Thomas met by chance one evening discovered that to be the case.

Early in his psychic career, Thomas gave readings at house parties. At one of those parties, he found himself offering information that was somewhat unusual.

"No one expects anything from a reading done at a house party," he said. "I ended up saying something negative that I would not usually say. I said, 'I don't know why I'm saying this to you, but don't go home tonight. I don't know why; just don't go home tonight.'"

This suggestion struck the recipient of the message as odd. Her husband and children were home. She asked if her family should be in the house, and Thomas replied that he didn't think they should be there either. The old house they were staying in had belonged to her husband's great-aunt who had passed away a few months before. They were living there temporarily until they could sell it.

The woman returned home, despite the warning, and didn't mention the reading to anyone.

"She slept on it that night, and the following day the reading lingered with her," he said. Finally, she shared it with her husband, who worked in finance on Wall Street. He was upset that she had kept it to herself. While the woman didn't put much credence in the reading, her husband, who'd had a psychic grandmother, took the warning quite seriously. He immediately rented a hotel room and moved the family into it.

The couple returned the following day without their children to assess whether there was something at the house they needed to address.

"He called his mom to talk about it. They decided that maybe they should get someone to inspect the house before the family returned."

The party had been Friday night; Saturday they had moved to the hotel.

"They were still at the hotel on Sunday, when a neighbor called them about five o'clock that evening. He said, 'Joe, where are you? There's a huge blaze coming out of your house.'" Faulty wiring had caused a rapid, intense fire on the second floor that might have killed or badly burned the family had they still been there.

The woman never forgot the experience.

"To this day she still sends me a Christmas card to say she is grateful that she has her family."

Dream Vacation

There may be several websites these days that offer sage advice on traveling, but Thomas has found that nothing compares to his own intuition. Several years ago he decided he wanted to visit Sedona, Arizona. He didn't want to stay in a hotel, so he investigated renting a house.

"I found this beautiful place," he said. The owner was going to be in Florida for several months and was renting out his house while he was gone.

The price seemed too good to be true, and the owner pressured him for a commitment, but Thomas told him that he wanted to think about it for a day. He was secretly concerned that the rent was lower than it should be. While this was a good thing for his budget, it made him feel cautious.

"He was a smart, cool guy in his late fifties or early sixties," Thomas said. He had no negative feelings about the man, but that night he had a dream.

"In my dream I went to the house, and there was a big hole in the ground where the house should have been. I called the owner the next day and said, 'I get

How has your unfolding psychic ability affected the way you treat other people, both those you know and strangers?

"It affects things because when I see people, I can see their past, present, and future around them. It gives me more empathy. I guess I also have more of an appreciation for what happens on the other side. They're still there to guide us. They can send us and show us love."

—Thomas

messages in my dreams. This is the dream I had. I don't know what it means, but I know that your rental is not for me.'"

About three weeks before his trip, Thomas spoke to the man again and discovered the rental was still available. The owner made him another offer.

"I said, 'No, I'm still going to pass,'" he said, opting to heed the warning he had received. It turns out that was a wise decision.

"The following week the man was killed in a motorcycle accident," he said. In the weeks that followed, several family members, including the dead man's sister, wife, and mother, descended on the house and began bitterly fighting over the property.

"If I had taken him up on this place, I would not have been able to stay there anyway."

Rev. Ilona Anne Hress, LCSW, LMT, Spiritual Healer/Teacher

On the Wing

Providing a loving home for a creature in need is truly a calling. Ilona has always been fond of birds and has several cockatiels that cheerfully greet guests as they enter her home. One special bird indelibly etched a place in her heart.

"I had Mei Mei for almost two years," Ilona said. Her winged friend was a white-faced pearl cockatiel. "She was a rescue bird. She came to me with a lot of respiratory and allergy problems."

Rev. Ilona Anne Hress and her rescue birds at home in Madison, New Jersey.

When Mei Mei arrived, she never left her cage, despite the fact that Ilona always kept the door open during the day as she did for her other birds.

"She was allergic to some of the toys in her cage and didn't groom

134

herself well," she said. "I ended up grooming her to teach her how." In addition to giving preening lessons, Ilona periodically cleared the bird's nostrils to help her breathe.

Because Mei Mei was so sickly, Ilona often had to administer antibiotics by syringe and perform energy healing to help bolster the bird's physical and emotional well-being. Her nurturing paid off.

"She became a diva," Ilona quipped. Mei Mei allowed anyone who came into the house to help preen her. She also came out of the cage a few times a day and began playing with the toys in her cage. She was learning to enjoy life.

Despite these breakthroughs, Mei Mei was never able to fully recover from her health problems.

"I learned that was just her. She came to me ill, and I did whatever I could." Most days Mei Mei was content to alight on Ilona's shoulder and observe her daily activities from that perch. They were constant companions.

Finally, the day came when Mei Mei's ill health caught up with her. When Ilona went to her cage one morning, she found the white cockatiel lying lifeless at the bottom.

"I think her little heart just gave out from having to breathe so hard," Ilona said. "I picked up her little body and preened it one last time."

That's when something unexpected happened. Ilona could see and feel Mei Mei flying around the room. When she buried Mei Mei near the house, the bird evolved even further.

"She became a ball of light and landed on my shoulder as she used to do in life," Ilona said. Mei Mei stayed with Ilona while she drove, when she showered, and as she slept.

A few days later, when walking through a park, Ilona spied a shiny, silvery light flickering in her peripheral vision.

"It was following us on the walk," she said. "I became aware that there was the spirit of a living bird who wanted to give birth to Mei Mei." Shortly after that, Mei Mei's spirit took flight.

"That little ball of light that had been on my shoulder moved right in front of my face. She was bursting with excitement and anticipation like a kid on Christmas. She flooded me with gratitude, appreciation, and joy." Mei Mei communicated to Ilona that she'd had a really great life, and then she flew off to experience her next one.

"It was truly joyous."

Jubilation

Ilona's aunt Anne, called Teti by most of the family, lived to be ninety-three years old. Her mother died when Teti was thirteen, leaving her to take care of her four brothers, a baby sister, and her father. It was the Great Depression, and like many families, hers often went hungry.

Teti never married but always offered loving support to everyone around her throughout her life. When the wife of one of her brothers died, she moved in to look after him.

"Part of the reason she lived to such a ripe old age was because she was so devoted to being there for her family," Ilona said. "She wouldn't sign a living will because of that commitment."

How old were you when you had your first psychic experience?

"It's always just been a part of me. When I was little, I would see things that nobody else saw. There was no one to go to … I saw forms and light. I also was aware that there were people, spirits, and some other dark things. I just learned how to deal with it. I began to manage it by myself at ten."

—Ilona

Eventually, her health failed and the live-in help called for an ambulance. The emergency technicians used extraordinary means to revive Teti, and she ended up on a ventilator.

Ilona and her brother were close to their aunt and went to visit her in the hospital.

"All the years I had known Teti, I had never seen fear in her eyes," she said. But now hooked up to a ventilator and not knowing what to expect, Teti was clearly afraid. Ilona performed energy work on Teti to try to allay her fears. Afterward, she left. What she didn't anticipate was that her aunt would follow her home.

"Even though my aunt stayed physically in the hospital bed, spiritually a big part of her auric field decided to come home with me," Ilona said. According to some belief systems, the physical body is surrounded by layers of auric fields, divided into five bodies, starting with the spiritual and ending with the physical.

Teti had gone to church all of her life, but Ilona said that her final days were a test of her faith.

"She began to wonder, 'Who is God? Where do you go? What happens?' She didn't know and was frightened. I meditated and started to explain what was happening. I explained chakras, and she witnessed my doing healings on all the people who came to my practice that week. I explained about the beauty of heaven." Then one night, while Ilona was meditating, her aunt went through Ilona's chakra column on her spine, out through her crown chakra at the top of the head, and saw her loved ones on the other side waiting for her.

"Literally, there was a party going on to meet her in heaven," she said. "There was her mother, her father, her friends, her aunts, and other people she had known in life. It was total jubilation." Teti's spirit left to join them.

Ilona knew it was just a matter of time before she got the call that her aunt had departed.

"It was graceful and it was easy. I was just screaming with joy for her. I knew that a big part of her had already left. There was no fear, just pure joy and love. She earned it." A week later, Teti physically died. There was no attempt to revive her. It was her time.

Chakras

Chakras come from the philosophy and practice of yoga in India and represent a tradition that is thousands of years old. In her book *Wheels of Life*, Anodea Judith describes chakras as seven wheel-like energy centers that rest along the spine. Their energy rotates in spirals much like miniature Milky Way galaxies. She adds that chakras are centers for receiving, integrating, and sending out our life energies. There are seven chakras, beginning at the bottom of the spine and ascending to the crown of the head. When energy flows freely through these chakras, then wellness is the result. If there is a blockage, then health can suffer. Acupuncture, shiatsu (a form of massage), and some traditional Asian medical systems are based on the chakras.

Dual Reality

At some point in life, most people experience the loss of a close friend. However, not everyone gets to experience a dual reality with them.

"Kay and I didn't talk to each other often, but when we did, it was always very poignant, and the connection was extremely deep," Ilona said. Whenever she needed help with life, Ilona would call Kay.

"She would consult her guides and relate what she heard," Ilona said. "Whatever she brought through for me was always right on the money, so I listened."

At the age of fifty, Kay died of a heart attack.

"Her partner called me at nine o'clock in the morning," Ilona said. "She had died in the middle of the night. At first I was shocked. Then the coolest thing happened. There is a life-review process that takes place immediately after you die. Your spiritual guides, your guardian angels, and your ancestors are there to help you to see what you accomplished and what you didn't accomplish and to help plan for your next incarnation. You also get to decide where you are going between now and your next incarnation to study and grow while still on the spiritual plane." She explains that only a part of the soul occupies the physical body; the rest always remains on the spiritual plane.

Ilona felt Kay's loss on the physical plane, but she simultaneously experienced being a part of her friend's support team on the other side.

"If you have cleared up enough of your karma, you don't have to reincarnate and can join the spiritual hierarchy to assist humanity," she said. Ilona had the chance to see Kay make that transition. Experiencing that dual reality left a lasting impression on her.

How do you think psychic abilities will be viewed in the future?

"Extrasensory perception of every kind is an evolutionary gift that will become the mainstream probably within a hundred years, or definitely within five hundred years. It is just the next level of communication. Psychic abilities are gifts and a blessing. Literally, with them we are using a new operating system to communicate."

—Ilona

"I missed the physical connection with her, but on the spiritual level I had participated in her evolution, so it was impossible to fall into grief."

Ethereal Therapy

Ilona said that the energies of the dead can remain on earth if they've suffered a trauma and getting them to leave a property should be done with care.

"Whenever I do ghost busting in homes, I'm having therapy sessions with discarnates, helping them with unfinished business," she said. "Kicking them out of a house just causes more residue." In this sense she considers herself a multidimensional counselor, drawing on her dual training as both a licensed clinical social worker and minister.

"Any home can be reclaimed if you're willing to listen to the stories of the people who have lived there," she said. "I always have to start by honoring the Native American Indians who were first on the land. Is there a problem there?"

Ilona currently lives in an old colonial home that has been divided into several apartments.

"I was here for three or four years before I used the basement on a regular basis," she said. "That's when I discovered the house was located on property that was a British redcoat encampment during the Revolutionary War." She involved the property owner, who was also psychic.

"We could sense the energy imprint of those who were ill, some with serious influenza," she said. "The cook and wife of one of the officers were in the basement. They had been ill and died there." She and her friend led the spirits, one by one, outside of the house. Then they began to see the encampment in more detail.

She said many of the soldiers were teenagers, not much older than fourteen. It was a terrible winter. Many people starved.

"I just said to them, 'Look, the United States and England are now allies. Sorry you lost the Revolution, but our countries came to peace. You get to go to heaven now. You don't have to be here anymore.' We asked for their loved ones to come and get them, and they all just lifted up into heaven. A deep peace entered the house and began to move into the stones in the basement. The land was reclaiming itself from war to peace."

Dead with Issues

Psychic medium Echo Bodine and psychic healer Rev. Ilona Anne Hress have suggested that the dead often have issues, not unlike the living. And because of that, they may hang around. Their reasons for lingering may include the belated urge to apologize for their behavior during life, a strong desire to let their loved ones know they're well, or the need to share what became of them if they were the victim of an untimely death or murder. These souls remain on earth until they see a resolution, and then they cross over.

Rev. James (Jim) E. DeBiasio, Spiritual Advisor

Guardians in the Hallway

Jim taught biology and chemistry at a private Catholic high school in New York for eleven years. From there he became a minister in a nondenominational church, a calling he has followed for the past thirty-six years. His Catholic upbringing reinforced his belief that guardians were always watching him. His personal experiences confirmed this.

When Jim was sixteen years old, he went to his high school after hours to help set up for a school dance. The other students hadn't arrived yet, so the long hallway where he was preparing the refreshments table was deserted. Normally, when people walked down that hallway, their footsteps would echo. So Jim was surprised when he looked up

Rev. James E. DeBiasio, a psychic medium and founder of the Institute for Spiritual Development who lives in Ft. Lauderdale, Florida.

and saw two people standing nearby. One was a young woman with long, blonde hair who wore a pink and white dress. She smiled sweetly at him. The other was an elderly man in a business suit. Jim greeted them both, and they struck up a conversation.

"They said something to the effect that my work in life would not be what I thought it would be," he said. At the time Jim was thinking of going to medical school.

"I turned around and they disappeared," he said. He felt puzzled but not at all disturbed. Then he forgot about it. The dance was about to start and his sixteen-year-old mind was more focused on the night's festivities.

The memory of that event returns to him now and again, but for quite some time he was not sure what to make of it.

"Years later I realized they were my spiritual teachers," Jim said. And they were right. He never did enter medical school, choosing instead to teach and eventually become a minister.

Guardian Angels

Guardian angels are a part of many cultures. Ancient Greeks referred to their spirit guardians as geniuses, which originally referred to the superior intelligence of all-knowing guardians. Egyptians referred to such beings as Ka, a protective divine being given to each person at birth. Early Judaism also believed in guardian angels for individuals, cities, and nations. The Roman Catholic Church has a Guardian Angel Society, and even Reverend Billy Graham has written about guardian angels. Islam acknowledges guardian angels as a blessing from God, sent to guide people through life. Guardians are also common in the Buddhist, Hindu, and earth-centered Native American religions.

Carnelian Affirmation

Requesting a tangible sign of a spirit guide, and then receiving it, is a rare event. Jim was fortunate enough to experience such an affirmation. It all began with a casual conversation.

In addition to teaching high school, Jim at one point also owned an antique store. One day a regular customer came by and chatted with him about a couple he knew who ran a weekly psychic development group.

"I expressed interest in the group, and he offered to introduce me to them," Jim said. "They, in turn, introduced me to the psychic world." The couple lived and conducted their classes in a roomy two-bedroom brownstone on the east side of Manhattan. "The husband was British and very charming," he said. "He was an actor." His wife had brown hair, a round face with soft brown eyes, and a pleasant disposition. Jim attended his first class out of curiosity. That night he went into a trance and gave a reading. From that point on, he was hooked, attending the class every week for the next twelve years.

"It was like coming home," he said. "The experience was incredibly familiar, like I had been going to the class for months or years."

Although Jim was intrigued, he had a sense of uncertainty about his abilities.

"On a personal level, you get into this work and then you have your period of doubt. You have your dark night," he said. "Is this really happening? Is it true?"

He attended a spiritualist camp in Pennsylvania, hoping to find out. He said to himself before he went, "If any of this is true, I'm going to get a sign, and that sign is going to be a cross." At the camp they conducted a materialization session, a deep meditation where objects would spontaneously materialize. During one such session, the smoky outline of a man appeared to Jim.

"One of my teachers materialized and said, 'Put out your hand.'" Jim did. At first he felt something warm in his hand, but nothing was there. "Then I felt a clunk, and a carnelian cross lay in my palm. I wore that cross for twenty-five years."

When he finally put the cross away in a jewelry box because he had stopped wearing it, the cross disappeared. Ten years later it reappeared in the same jewelry box, and he wore it again. It has disappeared and reappeared several times in his life.

The cross first came to him when he needed some tangible reassurance about his psychic abilities. He has long since ceased to doubt his gift or the spiritual world around him.

Earthbound Houseguest

Houseguests are notorious for overstaying their welcome. Jim remembered one time when someone from the other side came to visit—and stayed for quite a while. The unexpected guest was a good friend John, who was also the husband of one of his cousins.

John had been born with a heart condition and was ill most of his life. He and his wife lived two doors down from Jim, so John and Jim developed a close relationship.

"He was ill for a while and wasn't expected to live long," Jim said. John died in the hospital with his wife by his side. She had a particularly difficult time coping with the loss, which had some unintended consequences.

"His wife kept grieving and went to the cemetery every day. She even had lunch in the graveyard," Jim said. Quite simply, she couldn't let go of her beloved husband. As a result, John was unable to leave the earthly plane. Stuck on this side, John decided to take up residence in Jim's house.

"Her husband stood in the corner of my family room and didn't say anything," he said. "He just stayed there. I would come down for breakfast and say hi to him every day."

When you discovered your psychic ability, how did it alter the way you thought about the world around you?

"This goes back to the first day of Catholic school, when I was five years old. Our teacher began talking about angels. From that time forward I always knew that there were guardian angels. It just reassured me that what I had learned was actually real and true."

—Jim

Jim noticed that John's tall, gaunt frame was dressed in the same brown suit in which he had been buried. His form remained stationary, with a blank facial expression. He didn't speak. This went on for several years. Some people who visited Jim would see John standing in the corner and ask their host who it was.

"My house was a safe place for him to hang out while he waited for his wife to let go," Jim said. "He knew he would be seen and recognized here." But even on the spiritual plane, things change.

"I came down one morning and looked to say hello, and he had vanished. I realized that meant that his wife had emotionally let go of him." Jim was relieved and happy to know that, finally, both John and his wife could move on.

Stream of Consciousness

Sometimes when Jim is relaying messages during readings, the symbols he receives from the other side are not easy to interpret. This challenge presented itself once when he was onstage offering readings to a group of about 150 people.

"I got the impression of an American Indian for someone. I couldn't quite get his name. So he sent me the image of a dog peeing on a fire hydrant. I started laughing so hysterically, I couldn't get any words out." The image persisted for about five minutes. Finally, Jim understood the message: the Indian's name was Yellow Stream.

"Someone recognized the name and then I could do the reading."

Another such instance came during a private reading he gave a client in Florida.

How has your unfolding psychic ability affected the way you treat other people, both those you know and strangers?

"I think the great realization that comes from that type of awakening and connection to people on the intuitive level is that it puts meaning behind the words, 'We're all one; we're not separate.' I developed a strong sense of not judging and knowing that whatever someone else is going through is also part of my experience."

—Jim

"The woman was heavyset," Jim said. "I kept getting the image of her trying to crawl into a mailbox. Her head and hands were in the mailbox, and she was attempting to fit the rest of herself as well." He described this image to her and asked if it might mean anything. She gave it some thought and finally said no; the image didn't seem to connect with anything going on in her life.

When the session was nearly over, she asked him one last question: "Do you think I'm going to get the job in the post office?" He smiled. A week later she did.

Floating Coffins

Jim said that he occasionally receives a premonition of someone's passing. Two of Jim's clients were a mother and daughter from Pennsylvania. One day the mother, a woman in her sixties with salt-and-pepper hair, came by for a reading.

"She was a very sweet and gracious woman," he said. "And I believe she was retired. As she was walking out the door, I saw this image, and I said, 'I see all these little coffins floating around you.'" It was such a strange vision that Jim felt compelled to ask her about it. She replied that the image must be related to her sister. She had been quite worried about her health.

"Two weeks later her daughter contacted me," he said. "Her mother had rear-ended a truck and was killed. The truck was carrying a load of coffins."

CHAPTER 10

PEERING THROUGH
THE GATE TO ETERNITY

A primary reason psychic phenomena are hotly contested by the scientific community is that the validity of such phenomena would mean a major scientific revolution, similar to the Copernican revolution that forced us to accept the sun as the center of the solar system.

—Diane Hennacy Powell, MD, American psychiatrist/
former faculty, Harvard Medical School (~1955–)

Psychic Reflections

It would be reasonable to assume that having paranormal abilities—from occasional intuitive feelings to daily communication with the dead—might have an effect on how someone approaches life. Having contact with another dimension of reality has to expand a person's way of thinking. Many people do not admit to possessing such abilities, but those who shared their stories in this book obviously do. At the same time, many of them were reluctant to give their full names because they feared losing their jobs or being ridiculed—heavy penalties to pay for sharing an experience.

Perhaps most startling for me were the confessions I heard from many of the individuals I interviewed that I was the

Why do some people have such strong negative reactions to those who believe in psychic phenomena?

"It's a part of our Western scientific tradition that if something is not experientially proven, then it has no validity. Yet a psychic experience, being so subjective and personal in nature, runs counter to that paradigm. It's unique to the individual; others haven't shared it."

—Marcia

first person they had ever openly spoken with about their abilities, and having finally done so, for the first time in their lives, they felt comfortable and validated about their gift. Some of the people who told me this were middle-aged, so they had been yearning to talk to someone for a long time. I found myself wondering why psychic phenomena should be so taboo.

Beliefs are a powerful force in this world. Wars are fought over them. Cultures are ruled by them. They represent our core values in life and can even motivate someone to make the ultimate sacrifice. As a result, they are sacred and staunchly guarded. Perhaps that's why psychic phenomena can evoke such strong negative reactions. Paranormal events are very real to those who experience them and may seem like outrageous nonsense—sometimes blasphemy—to those who don't.

One situation that has always fascinated me is how paranormal activity can be vehemently attacked by both the scientific and religious communities, particularly at a time when efforts are being made to bridge those two camps. While taking courses to support my medical writing, I had a biology professor who dedicated an entire class period to explaining why, in his view, there was no conflict between science and religion. I recall being surprised, maybe even a bit put off, at the time. But in retrospect, I'm impressed that this intelligent and spiritual man was attempting this ideological reconciliation in the halls of scientific academia.

While religion has held sway in cultures since before recorded history, science is a relative upstart. In the seventeenth century, the scientific revolution heralded a new belief system in which theory had to be proven through reproducible experiments to be considered a fact. The general perception from that time forward was that science exclusively begat knowledge.

That way of thinking remains with us to this day, according to Matthew Ricard and Trinh Xuan Thuan in their book *The Quantum and the Lotus: A Journey to the Frontier Where Science and Buddhism Meet*. But science, they point out, is only a tool. It is not good nor bad nor all-knowing. And while the scientific method produces data, it does not produce wisdom. Science reveals insights that can transform our world, but only human experience and compassion can guide how. They conclude that "spirituality is not a luxury but a necessity."

Having grown up in the cultural wake of that strong scientific tradition, I was raised to believe that anything psychic was nothing more than ignorant superstition. So even if something remarkable occurred, it was dismissed as coincidence or childish imagination. Only upon reflecting back over the years can I discern the possibility of experiences that defy logical explanation. Because psychic phenomena tend to be related to personal perceptions that are challenging to measure or prove by Western scientific standards, they are often viewed as fantasy. That's what makes paranormal experiences so frustrating for those who wish to share them with a skeptical world. It's also what makes them so intriguing for those open to the possibility such things as clairvoyance and mediumship might actually exist.

Why do some people have such strong negative reactions to those who believe in psychic phenomena?

"I think everybody has a psychic experience at one time or another, even the most dyed-in-the-wool naysayers. What doesn't fit into your picture of the world, you can become very vehement about. After forty-five years of being involved in this, I am thoroughly convinced, and I've just let go of the notion that I have to convince anyone else. If you open yourself up to it, it will broaden your understanding of the world around you and of people. It's there for us to use."

—Jim

As an adult I have come to appreciate the point in *The Quantum and the Lotus* about science being tempered with wisdom. Science has greatly improved the longevity and quality of our lives by reducing disease mortality and providing us with many conveniences, including the computer I'm using to write this book. On the other hand, it has also given us pollution, the

atomic bomb, and a pace of life that can result in mental unrest. It is amusing to consider how corporate and governmental policies of the recent past might have turned out differently if boardroom and Congressional decision makers had only been aware of dead relatives nosily peering over their shoulders while they worked.

At the other end of the anti-psychic spectrum are those who are fearful of paranormal activity because they are concerned that it might be in conflict with their spiritual beliefs. They, of course, have the option to not read *Loitering at the Gate to Eternity,* and I respect their decisions in that regard.

My late mother-in-law was a devout Catholic who also happened to believe in psychic phenomena, because they were so common in her family. She saw no conflict between her spiritual beliefs and the invisible world around her. Indeed, most of the people I interviewed for this book are deeply spiritual. Their experiences have affirmed their beliefs rather than undermined them.

I'm not going to try to convince anyone of what they should or shouldn't believe. That would be absurd, and there are numerous more eloquent advocates of the paranormal out there, like J. B. Rhine, PhD, Louisa E. Rhine, PhD, Diane Hennacy Powell, MD, and Dean Radin, PhD, who have already written extensively on the subject. It's likely that our personal experiences and cultural beliefs will ultimately determine how we react to psychic phenomena anyway.

I hope you have found these tales entertaining and thought-provoking. It would be gratifying if, at the very least, these stories could launch an open-minded discussion about psychic phenomena for those who are as intrigued by them as I am.

References and Suggested Reading

Books

Anderson, George, and Andrew Barone. *Lessons from the Light: Extraordinary Messages of Comfort and Hope from the Other Side*. New York: Putnam, 1999.

Andrews, Ted. *How to Do Psychic Readings through Touch*. Woodbury, MN: Llewellyn Publications, 2005.

Artemidorus. *The Interpretation of Dreams: Oneirocritica*. Translated by R. White. Torrance, CA: Original Books, 2nd Edition, 1990.

Browne, Sylvia. *All Pets Go to Heaven: The Spiritual Lives of the Pets We Love*. Piatkus: London, 2010.

Cranston, Sylvia, and Carey Williams. *Reincarnation: A New Horizon in Science, Religion and Society*. New York: Julian, 1984.

Dossey, Larry. *The Power of Premonitions: How Knowing the Future Can Shape Our Lives*. New York: Dutton, 2009.

Greeley, Andrew M. *The Sociology of the Paranormal: A Reconnaissance*. Beverly Hills, CA: Sage Publications, 1975.

Guggenheim, Bill, and Judy Guggenheim. *Hello from Heaven: A New Field of Research (After-Death Communication) Confirms That Life and Love Are Eternal*. New York: Bantam, 1996.

Hill, Gary Leon. *People Who Don't Know They're Dead: How They Attach Themselves to Unsuspecting Bystanders and What to Do about It*. Boston: Weiser, 2005.

Johnson, Willard L. *Riding the Ox Home: A History of Meditation from Shamanism to Science*. Boston: Beacon, 1986.

Judith, Anodea, PhD. *Wheels of Life*. Woodbury, MN: Llewellyn Publications, 2008.

Klimo, Jon. *Channeling: Investigations on Receiving Information from Paranormal Sources*, 2nd ed. Berkeley: North Atlantic, 1998.

Lamoreaux, John C. *The Early Muslim Tradition of Dream Interpretation*. Albany: State University of New York, 2002.

MacLean, Kenneth James. *The Vibrational Universe: Harnessing the Power of Thought to Consciously Create Your Life*. Ann Arbor: Loving Healing, 2006.

Martin, Joel, and Patricia Romanowski Bashe. *Love Beyond Life: The Healing Power of After-Death Communications*. New York: Harper Collins, 1997.

Martin, Joel, Patricia Romanowski Bashe, and George Anderson. *We Don't Die: George Anderson's Conversations with the Other Side*. New York: G. P. Putnam's Sons, 1988.

McMoneagle, Joseph. *Memoirs of a Psychic Spy: The Remarkable Life of U. S. Government Remote Viewer 001*. Charlottesville: Hampton Roads, 2006.

Newton, Michael. *Journey of Souls: Case Studies of Life between Lives*. St. Paul: Llewellyn, 1994.

Powell, Diane Hennacy. *The ESP Enigma: The Scientific Case for Psychic Phenomena*. New York: Walker, 2009.

Prophet, Elizabeth Clare, and Erin L. Prophet. *Reincarnation: The Missing Link in Christianity*. Corwin Springs: Summit UP, 1997.

Radin, Dean I. *The Conscious Universe: The Scientific Truth of Psychic Phenomena*. New York: Harper Edge, 1997.

Rhine, Louisa E. *Hidden Channels of the Mind*. New York: W. Sloane Associates, 1961.

Ricard, Matthieu, and Xuan Thuan Trinh. *The Quantum and the Lotus: A Journey to the Frontiers Where Science and Buddhism Meet*. New York: Crown, 2001.

Rogo, D. Scott, and Raymond Bayless. *Phone Calls from the Dead*. Englewood Cliffs: Prentice-Hall, 1979.

Roland, Paul. *Explore Your Past Lives*. London: Godsfield, 2005.

Sargent, Denny. *Your Guardian Angel and You: Tune in to the Signs and Signals to Hear What Your Guardian Angel Is Telling You*. York Beach: Samuel Weiser, 2004.

Schmeidler, Gertrude Raffel. *Parapsychology: Its Relation to Physics, Biology, Psychology, and Psychiatry*. Metuchen: Scarecrow, 1976.

Stearn, Jess. *Edgar Cayce, the Sleeping Prophet*. Garden City: Doubleday, 1967.

Thompson, R., trans. *The Epic of Gilgamesh*. Oxford: Oxford University Press, 1930.

Tyrrell, G. N. M. *Apparitions*. London: Published under the Auspices of the Society for Psychical Research by G. Duckworth, 1953.

Van Praagh, James. *Ghosts Among Us: Uncovering the Truth about the Other Side*. New York: HarperOne, 2008.

Websites

Angier, Natalie. "Owls Start Coming Into Full View."*New York Times*, Accessed 25 Feb. 2013. http://www.nytimes.com/2013/02/26/science/long-cloaked-in-mystery-owls-start-coming-into-full-view.html?pagewanted=all.

"Brian Josephson's Home Page." University of Cambridge. Accessed 4 August 2012. http://www.tcm.phy.cam.ac.uk/~bdj10/.

Chisholm, Judith. "Electronic Voice Phenomena: Judith Chisholm Presents a Potted History of EVP." *ForteanTimes*. Dennis Publishing Limited, May

2005. http://www.forteantimes.com/features/articles/130/electronic_voice_phenomena.html.

"CIA-Initiated Remote Viewing at Stanford Research Institute." Institute for Advanced Studies. Accessed August 5, 2012. http://www.biomindsuperpowers.com/Pages/CIA-InitiatedRV.html.

"Consciousness and Physics." Boundary Institute. Accessed August 5, 2012. http://www.boundaryinstitute.org/bi/consciousness.htm.

"Consciousness Research Laboratory." Consciousness Research Laboratory. Accessed August 5, 2012. http://www.deanradin.com/CRL.htm.

"Do Dead People Watch Us? Yes, Author Says." *TODAY.com*. MSNBC Interactive, 17 July 2008. http://www.today.com/id/25724631/site/todayshow/ns/today-books/t/do-dead-people-watch-us-yes-author-says/#.USuET6WsiSp.

Frost, P. "Owls Mythology & Folklore." Raptors. 11 Apr. 2011. www.pauldfrost.co.uk

Hurkos, Stephany. "Peter Hurkos - Biography." Accessed August 5, 2012. http://www.peterhurkos.com/peter_biography.htm.

Jones, Steve G. "History of Out of Body Experiences."*Ezine @rticles*. Accessed 24 Feb. 2011. http://EzineArticles.com/5994368.

Josephson, Brian. "Lecture Collection." University of Cambridge. Accessed 4 August 2012. http://sms.cam.ac.uk/collection/664697.

Lachman, Gary. "The Occult World of CG Jung." *ForteanTimes*, Accessed 01 Mar. 2013. http://www.forteantimes.com/features/articles/3847/the_occult_world_of_cg_jung.html.

Marcot, Bruce G., David Johnson, and Mark Cocker. "The Spirit Chasers." *The Owl Pages*. Accessed 16 Feb. 2013. www.owlpages.com/articles.php?section=owl+mythology&title=owls+lore+culture&page=4.

"Overview." Institute of Noetic Sciences. Accessed 5 August 2012. http://www.noetic.org/about/overview/.

"Pet Statistics." ASPCA. Accessed 27 Feb. 2013. http://www.aspca.org/about-us/faq/pet-statistics.aspx.

"Premonition: Could Tapping Into Your Intuition Save Your Life?" Accessed 01 Mar. 2013. http://life.gaiam.com/article/premonition-could-tapping-your-intuition-save-your-life.

Rhine Research Institute Media Library: "70 Years at the Rhine." 30 Apr. 2012. http://www.rhine.org/media-library/sermon/52-70-years-at-the-rhine.html.

Schneider, Lisa. "Why the Dead Want Our Attention." *Psychic and Medium Echo Bodine Talks about Messages from the Dead in NBC's* Medium. Belief. net, 2005.. www.beliefnet.com/Wellness/2005/01/Why-The-Dead-Want-Our-Attention.aspx.

Smed, Jouni A. "Out-of-Body Experience Studies." The Monroe Institute, Accessed 16 Feb. 2013. www.monroeinstitute.org/resources/out-of-body-experience-studies.

"The Scottish School of Vibrational Medicine." The Scottish School of Vibrational Medicine. Accessed 19 Feb. 2013. www.scottishvibrationalmedicine.com.

"Types of Cases." University of Virginia School of Medicine, Division of Perceptual Studies. Accessed August 5, 2012. http://www.medicine.virginia.edu/clinical/departments/psychiatry/sections/cspp/dops/case_types-page.

"Webinar Series." International Consciousness Research Laboratories. Accessed August 5, 2012. http://icrl.org/basic-research/.

"Who We Are." University of Virginia. Accessed August 5, 2012. http://www.medicine.virginia.edu/clinical/departments/psychiatry/sections/cspp/dops.